EUROPEAN'S GUIDE TO GURKHALI

OR

(NEPALI GRAMMAR)

EUROPEAN'S GUIDE TO GURKHALI

OR
(NEPALI GRAMMAR)

A. W. CORNELIUS

GYAN

Published by

GYAN

Gyan Publishing House
5, Ansari Road
Daryaganj, New Delhi-110002
Phone: 011-47034999, 9811692060
E-mail: books@gyanbooks.com

Distribution Network
gyanbooks.com
India, USA, Canada, UK, Australia, France

ISBN : 978-81-212-4375-9 (PB)
First Published, 1944

2nd Impression 2020

Printed at: Gyan Press, Delhi.

European's Guide to Gurkhali
Author: A. W. Cornelius

Head Quarters, Meerut Dist.
Dehra Dun.*

31st December, 1942.

This is to certify that Mr. A. W. Cornelius has been employed by this District as an Army Language Teacher. He is a very experienced Urdu Instructor, extremely conscientious and thorough in all his work. We have received excellent testimonials about his good work from the officers he has instructed in Dehra Dun. I can thoroughly recommend him as a first-class Munshi.

In Dehra Dun, Mr. Cornelius has instructed in addition to numerous individual officers, classes at the following Units *5/2nd. Gurkha Rifles, 5/9th Gurkha Rifles, 17th British General Hospital* and at the *Survey of India.* They are extremely satisfied with his work.

G. J. Folkard
Major—A. E. C.
For Major General
Commander, Meerut Dist

PREFACE
to
"THE EUROPEANS' GUIDE TO GURKHALI"

The main object of writing this book is to help the British officers to acquire a good knowledge of the Nepali language. *Khaskhura* is the universal and common language of the inhabitants of Nepal.

The population of Nepal is mostly Hindus, known as *Gurkhas* and the language is called *Gurkhali*. It is, therefore, the best general dialect which can be learnt by the officers who are in the *Gurkha Regiments.* The following pages are intended to make the acquisition of this language easy to British officers. The present Grammar is more complete than any other yet written on this subject. The companion volume '*The English to Gurkhali Dictionary*' has been of great use in preparing this Grammar. By learning this language you will know and understand the people of Nepal better

In preparing this volume I owe a heavy debt of gratitude to Captain T. M. Hulse, 2nd Gurkha Centre, Dehra Dun. It is due, in a large measure, to his kindness and encouragement that the present work has been composed and printed.

Last, but not the least, the author is greatly indebted to Havaldar clerk N. B. Sinha, 2nd Gurkha Centre, Dehra Dun, for offering corrections and valuable suggestions.

I shall further appreciate all future help and suggestions that may be sent to me from time to time with a view to improving the *Second Edition* of this book.

Permanent Address:—
A. W. Cornelius
73, Chitwapur Road,
Lucknow, U. P.

9th May, 1944.

FOREWORD

'European's Guide to Gurkhali' is a timely publication for British officers and other persons, who are greatly interested to learn the Gurkhali language and need a Gurkhali Grammar in which they may find all the fundamental forms of language systematically arranged and explained. The author of this book has tried to fulfil the need of the British ofiicers; and has shown that the Gurkhali Grammar is most simple and easy to acquire.

I being a Gurkha, a trained teacher, and a Gurkhali tutor to many officers in the past, find that this is the best book of Grammar available in the market in my opinion.

Another very important feature is the fuller and better systematized explaination of the Grammar, supplemented by numerous exercises consisting of the words, phrases and expressions from every-day language.

I know, it will prove useful to any one working with no definite object in view except to acquire a good colloquial knowledge of *Khaskhura*, which is the most common language of the inhabitants of Nepal. According to my experience in the past, it is seen that different Gurkhali words are spoken in different Gurkha Regiments. But in this book the author has tried his best to keep to only one form i e the correct language spoken according to the Gurkha literatures of the present time.

Hav/Clerk—N. B. SINHA

9th May, 1944. 2nd Gurkha Centre, Dehra Dun.

TABLE OF CONTENTS
of
Nepali Grammar

Topics *Pages*

GURKHALI CONVERSATIONAL SENTENCES OF EVERY-DAY USE.

EUROPEAN'S GUIDE
To
GURKHALI

Abbreviations.

Trans	...	for Transitive Verb
Int	...	for Intransitive Verb
Adj	...	„ Adjective
Adv	...	„ Adverb
n	...	„ Noun
g	...	„ Garnu—to do
h	...	„ Hunnu—to be
f	...	„ Feminine
v	...	„ Verb

The Long Vowels

a (long) is like English "a" in Army, pass, father
i (long) is „ „ "i" in Police, machine
u (long) is „ „ "u" in Rule, too
e (long) is „ „ "e" in Say, belly, fate, pay
o (long) is „ „ "o" in Old, rope, go

The Short Vowels

a (short) is like English "a" in Woman, apart
i (short) is „ „ "i" in Bill, kiss
u (short) is „ „ "u" in full, pull

LESSON 1

ARTICLE

Nepali language has no regular article as the English *a* and *the*. The following words are used to represent the article in Nepali:--

Koī	...	Some, a certain
Yo	.	This
Tyo	...	That
Ek janā, ek, yeuṭā	...	One, a
Ti keṭāharu	...	The boys
Yeuṭā keṭo	...	A boy

LESSON 2

ORDINARY RULES FOR MAKING FEMININE

(a) The masculine nouns ending in a *Consonant*, add 'aī'

(b) The masculine nouns ending in a *Vowel*, the vowel is changed into, 'ai' 'i', 'nai'.

eg.	Chhoro (son)	...	Chhorī (daughter)
	Rājā (king)	...	Rānī (queen)
	Ghoṛā (horse)	...	Ghoṛī (mare)

Exception

1. Pāpī (sinner) ... Pāpinī (f)
2. Dās (slave) ... Dāsī (f)

LESSON 3

DECLENSION OF NOUNS.

	Singular		*Plural*
Nom.	Chhoro (son)	...	Chhorāharu (sons)
Agent.	Chhorole (by son)	...	Chhorāharule (by sons)
Genitive.	Chhoro kā. ko (son's)	...	Chhoraharuko, kā (son's)
Dative.	Chhorolāi (to a son)	...	Chhorāharulāi (to sons)
Accusative.	Chhorolāi (to son)	...	Chhoraharulāi (to sons)
Ablative.	Chhorobāta (from a son)	...	Chhorāharubāta (from sons)
Locative.	Chhoromān (in a son, on a son, upto a son)	...	Chhorāharumān (in sons)
Vocative.	E Chhorā (O ! son)	...	E Chhorāharu ho (O ! sons).

LESSON 4

IMPERATIVES.

In Gurkhali the Infinitive always ends in 'NU'; as gar-nu=to do. By dropping the 'NU' of the infinitive, the *root* or *stem* of a Verb is left, as gar=do, LI=take. Lekh=write.

IMPERATIVE FORMS.

There are four Imperative forms used in Nepali.

Imperative Forms of garnu=to do,

(1)	(2)	(3)	(4)
Gar (do)	Gar-a (do it)	Garnu (to do)	Garnu hos (Please do it, Will you please do it?)

1—Gar:--- is *impolite* and *abrupt* form of Imperative, hence it is seldom used.

2—Gar:-a--is used for giving *order* and *Command,* it is the one used in Military Units, eg.

Infinitive		Root	Imperative
Bhannu = to tell	...	Bhan ..	Bhana
Anu = to come	...	ā ...	āu

3—Garnu:- is politer than *Gara.*

4—Garnu hos:- is a very polite form of *Imperative.*

IMPERATIVE TENSE.

Garnu = to do.

Singular	*Plural*
1. M Gar-un	1. HamI gar-un
2. T Gar	2. TimI gar
3. Ū Gar-os	3. UnI gar-un

Useful Vocabulary

Answer	...	Jawāb
Are	...	Chhan
Bring	...	Lāu
Breakfast	...	Bihāna ko khānā
Bread	...	RoṭI
Book	...	Pustak, Kitāb
Clean (do)	...	Sāf garnu
Clean (Adj.)	...	Saf, Rāmro
Chair	...	KursI, Moṛā
Come	...	Āu
Come back	...	Farki āu
Carriage	...	GāṛI

Do	...	Gara
Dinner	...	Belka ko khānā
Door	...	Dhokā
Go	...	Jāu
Here	...	Yahān
Is	...	Chha
Letter	...	Chiṭṭhi
Make ready	...	Taiyār gara
Make	...	Banao
Milk	...	Dūdh
Place	...	Thāun
Put	...	Rākha
Ready	..	Taiyār

Useful Phrases.

Bring a rifle	...	Raifal liyau
Bring that book	...	Tyo kitāb liyau
Bring milk	...	Dūdh liyau
Bring hot water	...	Garam pānī liyau
Bring some sugar	...	Thoṛā chinī liyau
Clean the cap	...	Tyo ṭopī sāf gara
Come at 2, o,clock	...	Dui baje āu
Come in	...	Bhitra āu
Come here	...	Yahān āu
Come near	...	Najdik āu
Come soon	...	Jaldī āu
Come back	...	Farkī āu
Don't forget	...	Na bhulā
Don't come tomorrow	...	Bholi na āu
Give him my Compliments	...	Ūnlāi mero sewā dhok bhani dinu.
Give me some milk	...	Malāi alikati dūdh deu.

Exercise—1

Translate into English. (consult the 'Key')

1. Malāi ek kaṭorā chā deu. 2. Jaldī gara. 3. Aghāri or āiyanda eslāi na gara. 4. Eslāi wahāṉ na rakha. 5. Hallā na gara. 6. Daftar ma jāu. 7. Pathsālā ma āu. 8. Samāchār patra liyau. 9. Āj sānj ma āu. 10. Yahāṉ dekhi jāu.

Exercise —2

Translate into Gurkhali. (Consult the 'Key')

1. Come before six. 2. Come after four. 3. Go upto the river. 4. Hat is on the box. 5. Bring the parcel from the station. 6. He is in the room, open the door. 7. Put this on the bed. 8. Send for a tonga. 9. Call the tailor. 10. Shut this window.

Military Phrases

To attack	...	Hamla garnu
To advance	...	Aghi baṛnu
To imprison	...	Qaid garnu
To be killed	...	Marinu
To kill	...	Marnu
To be scattered	...	Tittar bittar hunu
To halt	...	*Halt* garnu *or* Rokinu
To besiege	...	Gher linu
To bombard	...	Golabārī garnu
To Capture	...	Pakrinu
To fire a gun	...	Bandūq parkaunu

LESSON 5

IMPERATIVE (Contd.)

Useful Vocabulary.

A little	...	Alik sano *or* alikati
All-right	...	Hunchha, Thik chha
Bath	...	Nohaunu
Butter	..	Nauni
Box	...	Bakas
Bad	...	Narāmro
Cold	...	Chiso, Jāro
Egg	...	Anḍā, ful
Good	...	Rāmro, Achchhā
Great	...	ṭhulo
Hot	...	Garam
Luggage	...	Sāmān
Many	...	Dherai
No	...	Nai, Chhaina, Hoina
Much	...	Dherai
Now	...	Aile
Open, (do)	...	Kholnu
Quickly	...	Chhito
Shut	...	Dhaknu, Band garnu
Soon	...	Chanro, Chhito
Small	...	Sāno
Tea	...	Chāha
Tomorrow	...	Bholi
Today	...	Āja
Thing	...	Chij
Table	...	Mej
Very	...	Dherai, Sarai

Water ... Pāni
Wait ... Thamnu
Window ... Jhiāl
Yes .. Ho, chha

Useful Phrases

Attack ... Jhaptinu
Bring me a cup ... Mero lāgi ek katora liyau
Bring my shoes ... Mero jutā liyau
Clean this table ... Yo mej sāf gara
Call the tailor ... Darji lāi bulāo
Close the gate ... Faṭak band gara
Do not go there ... Wahān̲ na jāu
Give it to me ... Yo malāi deu
Give it to him .. Yo uslāi deu
Go to the Post Office ... Dāk k̲h̲āne ma jāu
Go to the Doctor ... Doctor ko ma jāu
Is breakfast ready? ... Byāhāna ko khānā taiyār chha
Please don't come today ... Kirpa gari āj na āu
Show it to me ... Eslāi malāi dikhāu
Show it to him ... Eslāi ullāi dikhāu
Send it to him ... Eslāi usko ma pathau
Send it before 4 O'clock ... Eslāi chār baje dekhi pahile pathau.
Take it at cnce ... Eslāi chhito laijāu
Wait a little ... Alichhin aru thama

Exercise—3

Translate into English. (Consult the 'Key')

1. Malāi chakku aur kān̲ṭa deu. 2. Timro *boot* sāf gara. 3. Naukar lāi bulāo. 4. Nauni aur roṭi mej māthi rākha.

5. Timro *coat* ma burus gara. 6. Timro lugā sāf gara. 7. Lāṛai ma jāu. 8. Dhokā khola. 9. Cover gara. 10. Susta hinta.

Exercise—4

Translate into Gurkhali (consult the 'Key')

1. Send here. 2. Send out a patrol. 3. Put on the uniform. 4. Take off the clothes. 5. Arrest them. 6. Load the luggage on to this lorry. 7. Come to the city tomorrow morning. 8. Go to the bazar. 9. Come here (plural). 10. Come here.

Military Phrases.

To plunder ... Lūṭnu
To take a good aim ... Thīk nishānā lagāunu
To oil the rifle ... Raifal ma tel lagāunu
To fix the bayonet ... Sangīn lagāunu
You are responsible ... Timi zimmewār chhau
I think ... Mero bechār chha
Find out ... Khoja
I have heard ... Maile sune

LESSON—6

POSTPOSITIONS

Useful Vocabulary

According to ... Anusar
Along (with) ... Ko sang
At the side of ... Chheumān
After ... Ko pachhi

About (time)	... Punṛo
Before	... Ko agi, agāṛī
Before (time)	... Bhandā pahile
Below	.. Tala, muni, undho
Beside	... Paṭṭi, nira
Between	... Bīchmā
By means of	... Bāṭole
Besides	... Uprānta
Because of	... Kāraṉle
Concerning	.. Bishaymā
Before my house	... Mero ghar ko sāmne
From the direction of	... Bāṭo
For the sake of	... Garnu ko lāgi
From, since	... Dekhi, bata
In place of	... ṭhāuṉmā
In the middle of	... Māṉjhamāṉ
Inside of	... Bhitra, ko bhitra
In company of	... Sathmā
In return for	... Sāṭomā
In front of	... Sāmuṉne, aghāri
On, over, above	... Māṉthi
On the other side of	... Pāri, arko, Paṭṭi
Opposite to	... Sāṉmuṉne
Off	... Dur, taṛo
Outside	... Ko Bāhira
Outside of	... Bāira
On the side of	... Wāri
For	... Ko waste
Near	... Nira, najdik
Towards	: Tira
To, (place)	... Bhayeṭhāuṉ

Within ... Bhitra
With (at person) ... Sita
Of . Ko
Upon ... Ko māthi
From ... Dekhin, bāṭa
On ... Māthi
To ... Lāi
In ... Bhitra
Up ... Māthi

Useful Sentences.

Wait for him ... Usko lagi thama
His house is near the bazar... Usko ghar bajār nira chha
Of the man ... Mānchhe ko
Upto the river ... Kholā samma
In the room ... Kothā mā, kamra bhitra
From the office ... Daftar dekhi
On the box ... Baks māthi
To the school ... Pāṭhsala ma
Out of the range ... *Range* dekhin bhāira
To go on rounds ... Chakkar lagānu
Under the command of ... Hukm ko tala
They fled in all directions .. Uni haru chārai disa ma bhāgi gaye
The book is on the table ... Postak mej mānth chha
The book is beneath the table ... Pustak mez muni chha
How far up is Mussoorie ... Mussoorie kati mānthi chha
He spoke to me ... Ma sita bhanyo
He went from me ... Ma bata gayo
To his house ... Usko ghar tira

From our house	...	Hāmro ghar dekhi
In the Garden	...	Phulbāri ma
Under the table	...	Mej muni
In which direction	...	Kun patti
In the evening	...	Sānjh ma

N. B. 'Ko' is not used with it, only *Nira or Najdik* are used

'To' used for a place='mā': He went to Mussoorie = Tini Mussoorie mā gaye.

'To' used for a thing: He went to the house = Uni ghar mā gaye.

Exercise—5

Translate into English. (consult the 'Key')

1. Es shahr ko nām kye ho? 2. Bhartī hunu bhanda aghī kye kām garthyau? 3. Jab ma bajar ma thiyen. 4. Camp yahān dekhi kati tāro chha? 5. Sahib ko banglā kun ho? 6. Pallo paṭṭi kye chha? 7. Yos ko dām kati ho?

Exercise—6

Translate into Gurkhali. (Consult the 'Key')

1. Inside the house. 2. At my place. 3. They will wait for you. 4. These soldiers will go on route march. 5. Our planes will drop bombs on the enemy. 6. We will go to C.O. at 10, o'clock. 7. A section will take up a position on the hill. 8. They may be in that tant.

LESSON 7

PRONOUNS.

Declensions of Pronouns.

(First Personal Pronoun)

Singular		*Plural*	
I	... Ma	We	... Hāmiharu
Me	... Malai	Us	... Hāmiharulāi
To me	... Malāi	To us	... Hāmiharulāi
By me	... Maile	By us	... Hāmiharule
My	... Mero, Mera, Meri.	Our	... Hāmiharuko, kī, kā.
In me	... Ma mā	In us	... Hāmiharumā

(Second Personal Pronoun)

Singular		*Plural*	
Thou	... Tan	You	... Timiharu
Thee	... Tanlāi	You	... Timiharulāi
To thee	... Tanlāi	To you	... Timiharulai
By thee	... Tainle	By you	... Timiharule
Thy	... Tero, terī, terā	Your	... Timiharuko, kī, kā.
In thee	... Tanmā	In you	... Timiharumā
O thou	... Etan		

DECLENSION OF PRONOUNS

Singular

Pronouns	Nominative	Agent	Genitive	Dative	Accusative	Ablative	Locative
I	M	Maile	Mero	Mlāi	Mlāi	Mbāta	M mā
Thou	T	Tainle	Tero	Tlāi	Tlāi	Tbāta	Tmā
He, She	U	Usle, ulle	Usko	Uslāi	Uslāi	Usbāta	Usmā
This	Yo	Yesle	Yesko	Yeslāi	Yeslāi	Yesbāta	Yesmā
That	Tyo	Tesle	Tesko	Teslāi	Teslāi	Tesbāta	Tesmā
Who	Jo, ko	Jasle, jalle	Jasko	Jaslāi	Jaslāi	Jasbāta	Jasmā
What	Kye	...	...	...	...	...	...
Some one, Any one	Koi, kun	Kasaile	Kasaiko	Kasailāi	Kasailāi	Koibāta	Kasmā
Honorific Your honour	Āfu	Āfule	Āfnu	Āfulāi	Āfulāi	Afubāta	Āfumā
Reflexive Self	Āfai	...	...	...	...	...	...

N. B. T = tan

Form of 'ko' is as 'koi' in other forms.

DECLENSION OF PRONOUNS

Plural

Pronouns	Nominative	Agent	Genitive	Dative, Accusative	Ablative	Locative
We	Hamiharu	Hamiharule	Hamiharuko	Hamiharulāi	Hamiharubata	Hamiharuma
You	Timiharu	Timiharule	Timiharuko	Timiharulāi	Timiharubata	Timiharuma
They	Uniharu	Uniharule	Uniharuko	Uniharulāi	Uniharubata	Uniharuma
These	Iniharu	Iniharule	Iniharuko	Iniharulāi	Iniharubata	Iniharuma
Those	Tiniharu	Tiniharule	Tiniharuko	Tiniharulāi	Tiniharubata	Tiniharuma
Who	Junharu	Junharule	Junharuko	Junharulāi	Junharubata	Junharuma
What	...	...	...	...	..	Same as singular
Some one, Anyone	...	...	...	...	..	
Honorific Your honour	...	...	...	...	...	
Reflexive Selves	Āpāstmā	...	...	...	...	

'N. B.' Jo and Jun, both are singulars.
Koi and Kun, „ „ „

Useful words.

Call	...	Bulāunu
This	...	Yo
Count	...	Ginnu
That	...	Tyo
Clothes	...	Lugā
Who	...	Ko?
Distinctly	...	Safāile
What	...	Kye?
Fork	...	Kāṇṭā, khānā ko lāgi
Give	...	Diṇu
Groom	...	Sais—Ghoṛā wālā
Who	...	Ko, Jo
Horse	...	Ghoṛā
When	...	Kaile?
Office	...	Daftar
Why	...	Kina?
Loudly	...	Jorle
When	...	Jaba
Slowly	...	Sustale
Which	..	Kun?
Send for	...	Bolāuṇu
Like that	...	Tyesto
Tell	...	Bhanna
Like this	...	Esto
Come now	...	Aile āye
Whose	...	Kasko
Some way	...	Katai
Where	...	Kahāṇ, kata
Anywhere	...	Kahīṇ, jatāsukai
Here	...	Yahāṇ, eta

There	...	Tyahāṉ.
In that way	...	Tyeso, Tesari.
How	...	Kati?
How many	...	Kati?, Kati-watā?
Who came	...	Ko āye?, Ko ayo?
Which one	...	Kun chaiṉ, Kun.

Exercise—7

1. Ū hāmra ghar dekhi āye.
2. Ū ghar ko cheo ma thiyo ?
3. Ū lekhnu māngchhan.
4. Sahr ko bāṭo kata ho ?
5. Yahāṉ basyeko kati din bhayo ?

N B. 'Kun'—is more honorific than 'Ko
'Ke'— is sometimes used for 'Kye'

Exercise—8

1. He does not go to the lines every day.
2. If you start now, you will arrive there at 8:30.
3. If he is ill, he will not come.
4. I will send the book tomorrow.
5. We shall go to the bazar.

LESSON 8

PRESENT SUBJUNCTIVE OR AORIST TENSE.

The present Subjunctive tense is formed from the root by adding the personal terminations.

Conjugation of To do—garnu.

Singular

1. I may do it ... Ma gar-ne thyen.
2. Thou mayst do it .. Tainle gar-ne thyis.
3. He may do it ... Ulle gar-ne thyo.

Plural

1. We may do it ... Hamile gar-ne thiyuṉ
2. You may do it ... Timile gar-ne thiyoū
3. They may do it ... Unle gar-ne thye

Useful Sentences

If he works hard ... Agar usle parishrm garos.

If they like ... Agar uniharule chāhun.

I may see ... Ma dekhūṉ.

I may go ... Ma jāūṉ.

I may write ... Ma lekhūṉ.

If he comes ... Agar ū āos.

If we people go ... Agar hamiharu jāūṉ.

He might go to-day ... Kadāpi ū āj jāos.

May we go to the station? ... Hami station jāūṉ?

If you start now, you will arrive there at 8: 30. ... Agar taṉ aile hiṛlas ta saṛhe āṭh baje wahāṉ pugne chhas.

Should you tell me this I would be pleased. ... Taṉ malāi yo bhanthis ta ma khus hune thiṉyeṉ.

Possibly he might come today. ... Sāyad ū āj āus.

If you observe that ground, it would be better ... Agar taṉ tyo jamin dekh this ta jāti hune thiyo.

If it is raining don't go to *Mussoorie* ... Agar barkhā hudai rahyo ta *Masuri* na iānu.

LESSON 9

SIMPLE FUTURE TENSE.

Conjugation of To do—garnu:

Singular

1. I will do it ... M gar-unla
2. Thou wilt do it ... T gar-las
3. He will do it ... Usle gar-la

Plural

1. We will do it .. Hamīharu gar-ũnla
2. You will do it . Timīharu garaula
3. They will do it ... Unīharu gar-lan

Useful words.

Pursue ... Pichhā
Tomorrow ... Bholī
Tea ... Chāha
Letter ... Patra
Post ... Dāk
Sleep .. Sutne
To night ... Ȧja rāti

Future of Verb 'to be':

Singular

I will be .. M hunchhu
Thou wilt be ... Taṇ hunchhas
He will be ... U hunchha

Plural

We will be ... Hamiharu hunchhaũn
You will be . Timiharu hunchhau
They will be ... Uniharu hunchhan

Short Sentences

It is possible. ... Yo munasib chha, Hunchha hola
Clear this tent. .. Yo tambū khāli gar
Have you fresh eggs? .. Kye timi sanga tāja phul chha?
Is it dangerous? .. Tes ma khatra chha ki?
Stop the Lorry ... Lārī lāi roknu
What is the Railway fare ... Rel ko kirāyā kati lāg chha?

Useful Sentences

1. They will pursue the enemy ... Ūni haru dusman ko pichhā garlan.
2. I will go tomorrow ... Ma bholī jāunlā
3. You will take cover behind the hill ... Tan ū pahaṛ ko pichhāṛī lukera baslas.
4. Our regiment will be stationed in this Cantonment ... Hāmro palṭan yo chhauni mān baslā.
5. Will you have tea? ... Tan chāhā khanchhas?
6. She will write a letter ... Ūlle eota patra lekhli
7. He will come from the station ... Ū station dekhin ālā
8. John will give the book tomorrow .. John le kitāb bholi delā
9. I shall pay all the servants at 9: o'clock ... Ma 9 baje sab naukar harulāi paisā diunla.
10. He will send the answer by post ... Ūsle jawāb ḍāk bāta pathālā.
11. I shall write a long letter .. Ma eoṭa lāmo chiṭṭhī lekhunlā
12. Where will you sleep tonight ? ... Aja rāti tan kahan sut chhas ?

LESSON 10

PRESENT IMPERFECT TENSE.

Conjugation of To do=garnu.

Singular

1. I am doing ... M gar-dai chhu
2. Thou art doing ... Tan gardai chhas
3. He is doing ... Ū gardai chha

Plural

1. We are doing ... Hamīharu gardai chhaun
2. You are doing ... Timiharu gardai chhau
3. They are doing ... Unīharu gardai chhan

Useful words

No ... Hoina, nai
Writes ... Lekh chha
Language ... Bhāsa
At what time ... Kati baje
Aero-plane ... Hawā-jahāj
Well or good ... Rāmro
Learn ... Sikhnu
Always ... Sandāi

Useful Sentences

1. Do you know this language? ..Kya tan yo bhāsa jānda chhas?
2. At what time do you go to your Office. ... Kati baje tan āfno daftar janchhas?
3. I do not play football, I play Hockey ... Man golā kheldina, hāki khel chhu.

4. Our aero-planes fly over this area daily	... Hāmro hawā-jahāj yo hāta māthi roj urda chha.
5. Where does the Subedar live?	... Subedar kahān baschhan?
6. He is coming from Benares ..	Ū Benares (Kāshi) dekhi āundai chha.
7. He speaks and writes Gurkhali well	... Ū Gurkhali rāmrari bolchha ani lekh chha.
8. I live in a small city called Roorkee	... Ma Roorkee bhanne sāno sahar mān bas chhū.
9. These recruits learn Roman Urdu	... E rangruṭharu Roman Urdu sikhdai chhan.
10. I always get up early in the morning	.. Ma sandāi bihāna chānrai uṭh chhu.

LESSON 11

PAST CONJUNCTIVE PARTICIPLE.

Having gone	... Gaye pachhi *or* g e-ra.
Having seen it	... Here-ra, dekhe-ra.
Having done it	... Gar-ikana *or* garera.

Useful Sentences

1. I will write a letter and give it to the peon	... Ma ch ṭṭhi lekhera peon lai di diunlā.
2. He comes to my room and writes the letter	... Ū mero kothā mān āe ra chiṭṭhi lekh chha.
3. Go to the bazar and bring these things	... Bajar gae-ra yo chijharu lāu.
4. I will go and find out, what is the matter ?	... Ma gae-ra patā lagāunlā ki kye bhayo ?

5. Go to your company Commander and tell him there will be no parade this evening .. Āfno Company Commander lai gae-ra bhana ki āj sām *parade* hune bhhaina.

6. Load all this luggage and take it to the Station .. Sab sāmān motor gaṛī mān lāde-ra *station* ma lāi jāu.

7. Fold up the clothes and put them away ... Sab lugā pat-tiyāye-ra rākhi deu.

8. Having wept he said ... Ūlle roe-ra bhaneo.

9. C O. having heard this, became very angry ... C.O. Sāhible yo kura sune-ra sarai naraj bhaye.

10. Kindly listen to what I have to say ... Kirpā gare-ra mero binti suni leu.

LESSON 12

CONJUGATION OF THE *AUXILIARY VE B*

We shall now proceed to give the *Conjugation of the Auxiliary Verb* Hunu = to be *or* to become.

(a) THE IMPERATIVE.

Singular	*Plural*
1. Ma hun	1. Hamīharu hoūn
2. Tyo ho	2. Timiharu hau
3. Ū hawas	3. Unīharu hun *or* hoūn

(b) THE FUTURE.

Singular

1. Ma hunchhu *or* hunla .. I will be.
2. Yo hunchha *or* hola .. Thou wilt be.
3. Ū hunchha *or* hola ... He will be.

Plural *

1. Hamiharu houn̲la ... We will be.
2. Timiharu hunchhau *or* haula... You will be.
3. Uniharu hunchhan *or* hunan .. They will be.

(c) PRESENT IMPERFECT TENSE.

Singular

1. M hun̲da chhu *or* hun ... I am
2. Tan̲ chhas *or* hos ... Thou art
3. Ū chha *or* ho ... He or she is

Plural *

1. H chhaun̲ *or* houn ... We are
2. T chhau *or* hoū ... You are
3. Ū chhan *or* hun ... They are

(d) PAST ABSOLUTE TENSE.

Singular

1. M Thiyen̲ *or* Bhāyen ... I was
2. Tan̲ Thiyis *or* Bhāis ... Thou wast
3. Ū Thyo *or* Bhāyo ... He was

Plural *

1. H Thiyeun̲ *or* Bhāyeun... We were
2. T Thiyau *or* Bhāyau ... You were
3. U Thiye *or* Bhāye ... They were

(e) PRESENT PERFECT TENSE.

Singular

1. M Bhāyeko chhu .. I have been
2. T Bhayeko chhas .. Thou hast been
3. Ū Bhāyeko chha .. He has been

* In Plural forms, H=Hamiharu.
T=Timiharu.
U=Uniharu.

*Plural**

1. H Bhayeka chhaun ... We have been
2. T Bhayeka chhau ... You have been
3. U Bhayeka chhan ... They have been

(f) PAST PERFECT TENSE.

Singular

1. M bhāyeko thyen ... I had been.
2. T bhāyeko this ... Thou hadst been.
3. Ū bhāyeko thyo ... He had been.

*Plural**

1. H bhāyeka thyaun ... We had been.
2. T bhāyeka thyau ... You had been.
3. U bhāyeka thiye ... They had been.

(g) FUTURE PERFECT TENSE.

Singular

1. M bhāyeko hunla ... I must have been.
2. T bhāyeko holas ... Thou must have been.
3. Ū bhāyeko hola ... He must have been.

*Plural**

1. H bhāyeka hounlā ... We must have been.
2. T bhāyeka houla ... You must have been.
3. U bhāyeka holān ... They must have been.

*In Plural forms, H = Hamiharu
T = Timiharu
U = Uniharu

MISCELLANEOUS EXERCISES

Exercise—9

Translate into Gurkhali. (Consult the 'Key')

1. Go to your barrack. 2. Give it to him. 3. Go to my house 4. Where is Jit Bahudar? 5. Let me know as soon as the C. O. comes. 6. Write in my book. 7. Think before you answer. 8. Do you drink tea every day? 9. Where does the Hawaldar live? 10. He does not live here. 11. He lives in the lines. 12. What is the number of his house? 13. Where will you go now? 14. I will go to the Office. 15. We shall go there this evening.

Exercise—10

Translate into English. Consult the 'Key')

1. Ule ke bhandai chha? 2. Yo ke ko lagi chha? 3. Arko manchhe lai pathai dinu. 4. Furti manchhe chha? 5. Aba sun. 6. Yo kamra ko chhat chuhunchha. 7. Kasko palo ho chha? 8. Bhinnai bhinnai khal ko sawal sodhnu. 9. Yo ghisi sakyo. 10. Nikli jau.

LESSON 13

THE PAST TENSE.

The Past Tense is formed by adding 'yo' to the root.

Infinitive	*Root*	*Past Tense.*
Bolnu	bol	bol-yo, (spoke).
Lekhnu	lekh	lekh-yo, (wrote)
Paṛhnu	paṛh	paṛh-yo, (read).
Linu	li	lagyo, (took).
Dinu	di	di-yo, (gave).

The list of Irregular Verbs.

1. Gayo—Went, 2. Bhayo—became, 3. Gareyo—did, 4. Maryo—died.

Useful Sentences.

1. I gave the person a rupee ... Manchhe lāi ek rupiyā diyen.
2. I told you before ... Māile timi lāi aghinai bhanyen.
3. He did it knowingly ... Usle jāni bhuje garyo.
4. The boy came ... Keto āyo.
5. The boy did it ... Ketole garyo.
6. He abused ... Usle gali diyo.
7. He spoke to me ... Ū ma sita bolyo.
8. He gave the son a book .. Usle chhorolāi eyota pustak diyo.
9. When did he come? ... Tiyo kaile āyo.
10. He asked me ... Usle ma sita sodhyo.
11. I went ... Ma gayen.
12. He saw it ... Usle dekhyo.

Exercise—11

Translate into English. (Consult the 'Key')

1. Usle afnai khusi le garyo. 2. Usle malāi ek roṭi diyo. 3. Tiyo kahile āyo. 4. Usle na jāni garyo. 5. Maile madān jang ma bahudari garen. 6. Uni harule āja āṭh baje bihanā drill khele. 7. Jamadar Sāhib le bhane ki jawan harule khānā khāyo. 8. Hijo usle apno sabaq paṛhena. 9. Hijo rati sute na. 10. Usle dekhiyo.

Exercise—12

Translate into Gurkhali. (Consult the 'Key')

1. I went to the Station at 5, o'clock. 2. At what time did you arrive Yesterday? 3. Who brought this letter

4. How long did you stay in Mussoorie? 5. Where did you go in the morning? 6. Mr. John stayed a week in Lucknow. 7. Who brought this letter from H. Q.? 8. Why did you not come at 9:15? 9. The Urdu teacher did not come today. 10. How many soldiers went on leave?

LESSON 14

Āfu=you. (Respectful).

We use āfu for respect to a gentleman and ladies, never use Timi *or* Tan.

1. How are you?...Āfu kasto hunū hun chha?(respectful) Timi kasto chhau. (ordinary)
2. Subedar Sahib what is your name? ... Subedār Sāhib āfu ko nam kye ho?

Āf=Self.

1. He saw his own book ... Usle āfno pustak dekhyo.
2. He saw *his* book ... Usle usko pustak dekhyo. (*his* means some one else)

To translate the English word 'To' *means* 'Ko pās' *or* 'ma'.

1—When 'to' refers to animate objects, it is translated 'ko pās' with Verb of motion, like āunū—To come, Jānu—To go, Laijānu—To take away, Liāunu--To bring.

eg. (a) Go to him ... Usko pās jāu.
(b) Go to the tailor ... Darjī ko pās jāu.
(c) Go to the C. O. ... C. O. Sāhib ko pās jāu.

2--When 'to' refers to inanimate Objects, it is translated by 'ma'.

eg. (a) Go to the Post Office ... Dāk khāna ma jāu.
(b) Go to the Office ... Daftar ma jāu.
(c) Come to the house ... Ghar ma āu.

Verb 'to have' is expressed in many ways.

(a) John has a horse ... John ko pās ma ghoṛā chha.
(b) John had a horse ... John ko pās ma ghoṛā thiyo.
(c) I have one sister ... Mero ek baini chhā.
(d) I have fever ... Hamilāi bukhār chhā.

N.B.—Thiyo or Theo;—both are Commonly used.

LESSON 15

THE POSSESSIVE CASE.

The possessive caṣe in Nepali is expressed by using '*ko*' only in Masculine gender. (In Gurkhali kā, ke are not used like Hindustani).

eg. (1) The man's house ... Manchhe ko ghar.
(2) The man's horses ... Manchhe ko ghoṛāharu.
(3) On the men's house ... Manisharu ko ghar mathi.
(4) On the men's horses... Maṇisharu ko ghoṛā haru mathi.

For feminine 'kī' is used, when the object possessed is feminine.

eg. (1) The man's mare ... Manchhe kī ghoṛī.
(2) The man's mares ... Manchhe kī ghoṛīharu.

Use of Na

1—In Nepali 'Na' is used to show *strong Negative Future.*

eg. Ū jā ne bhaina ... He will not go at all.

2—'Na' is used in all the Compulsive forms.

eg. (1) You ought not to do it ... Timilai garnu chāhinna.
(2) You must do it ... Timilai garnu chāhin chha.
(3) You had to do it ... Timilai garnu paṛeo.

Phrases.

Kaile-na-kaile	... Sometime *or* other.
Kahin-na-kahin	... Somewhere *or* other.
Koi-na-koi	... Some one *or* other.
Kei-na-kei	... Something *or* other.

LESSON 16

THE PRESENT PERFECT TENSE

The Present Perfect Tense is formed by adding the Present Tense of the Auxiliary Verb 'hunu' = to be, to the Past Participle of the main Verb.

Singular

1. Maile lekhe ko chhu	... I have written.
2. Timile lekhe ko chha	... You have written.
3. Usle lekhe ko chha	... He has written.

Plural

1. Hamiharule lekhe ka chhaun	... We have written.
2. Timiharule lekhe ka chhau	... You have written.
3. Uniharule lekhe ka chhan	... They have written.

N.B. 'Timi'—is used in singular as well as plural. But the correct word for plural is 'timiharu;' ie when 'haru' is used either after a noun or pronoun (in most cases) it becomes automatically plural.

Useful Sentences.

1. I have written a letter ... Maile chiṭṭhi lekhe ko chhu.
2. He has seen a book ... Ūsle pustak dekhye ko chha.
3. He has gone to the station .. Ū *station* gaye ko chha.
4. Have you seen our Platoon ..Hamro *Platoon* dekhiyau ki.

Exercise—13

Translate into Gurkhali. (Consult the 'Key')

1. They have gone to the station. 2. Have you written a letter to England? 3. She has gone to Miss Helen's place. 4. I have seen Mr. John. 5. Has he brought an answer? 6. Have you brought my lugguage from the station? 7. He has gone on leave. 8. Has the tailor come?

Exercise—14

Translate into English. (Consult the 'Key')

1. Colonel Sahible hija 'Inspection' garye. 2. Hamiharule bahut dushman ko sāmna gariuṉ. 3. Uniharu 5 ghanṭa ma 15 *mile* hiṉṛe. 4. Āja hamiharule bihāna 10 baje khānā khāye ko thiuṉ. 5. Jawānharule āfno sabai kām bhiāi sakye. 6. Timile bayān suneu. 7. Hami rupiya harāyeko chhu. 8. M āyeko chhu. 9. Hamro fauj dekhyau ki. 10. Delhi gayeko chha hola. *11. Ū gaye ko chha.

N. B. 'le'*—is not used with Intranstive Verbs.

LESSON 17

THE PAST PERFECT TENSE.

The Past Perfect Tense is formed by adding the Past Tense of the Auxiliary Verb 'hunu' = to be, to the Past Participle of the main Verb.

Singular

1. Maile lekhe ko thinyen ... I had written.
2. Timile lekhe ko thiyo ... You had written.
3. Usle lekhe ko thiyo ... He had written.

Plural

1. Hamiharule lekhe ka thinun ... We had written.
2. Timiharule lekhe ka thiyoū ... You had written.
3. Uniharule lekhe ka thiye ... They had written.

Useful Sentences.

1. He had seen it ... Usle dekhe ko thiyo.
2. We had written a letter... Hamiharule chiṭṭhi lekhe ke thinun.
3. I had gone ... Ma gaye ko thiyen.

N. B. No 'Le' is used with the following words.

1. Bolnu ... to speak. 2. Laṛnu ... to fight.
3. Lānu ... to bring. 4. Daṛnu ... to fear.
5. Lai jānu...to take away. 6. Birsinu... to forget.
7. Lagnu .. to take. 8. Milnu ...to find, to meet
9. Pugnu... to reach. 10. Bujhnu...to understand.

Exercise—15

Translate into Gurkhali. (Consult the 'Key')

1. I had seen him Yesterday. 2. He had arrived two days ago. 3. There had been a storm yesterday. 4. He had studied for six months. 5. They had written a long letter to England. 6. John had given a book to Henry. 7. They had eaten (taken) their food. 8. He had seen it.

Exercise—16

Translate into English. (Consult the 'Key')

1. Hamro manchhe harule *trench* khāne ko thiyo. 2. Colonel Sahib le razā manjūr gare ko thiyo. 3. Gurkhali Palṭan Burma mā khub laṛe ko thiyo. 4. Bavarchī le Khānā pakai rakhe ko thiyo. 5. Maile uslai Bombay ma dekhe ko thiyen.

LESSON 18

PAST IMPERFECT TENSE.

Singular

1. M gar-dāi thyen ... I was doing.
2. T gar-dāi this ... Thou wast doing.
3. U gar-dāi thiyo ... He was doing.

Plural

1. Hamiharu gardāi thiyaun ... We were doing.
2. Timiharu gar-dāi thyau ... You were doing.
3. Uniharu gar-dāi thye ... They were doing.

Short Sentences.

1. He was seeing ... Ū dekhdāi thiyo.
2. He was going to Station ... Ū *Station* jāndāi thiyo.
3. I was writing a letter ... Ma chiṭṭhi lekhdāi thyen.
4. We were speaking ... Hamiharu bāt gardāi thiyaun.
5. They were speaking ... Ūniharu bāt gardāi thye.

N, B. (1) Root + dāi = Present Participle.

(2) Present Participle + Auxiliary = Past Imperfect Tense.

(3) When 'dāi' is added to a root, after taking out 'Nn' from it, it always becomes continuous Tense.

Infinitive	*Root*	*Imperfect tense.*
Garnu	Gar	Gar-dāi. (doing)
Sutnu	Sut	Sut-dāi. (sleeping)
Hiṛnn	Hiṛ	Hiṛ-dāi. (going)

Exercise—17

Translate into English. (Consult the 'Key')

1. Ū sandāi nayā samachār lāu thiyo. 2. Hamiharn ghayal haru lāi aspatāl lāi jān thiun. 3. Hamro jawān yo maidān mān pareḍ gardāi thiye. 4. Uniharu kye kye khel khelda thiye. 5. Dui sāl aghi hanū ek ṭhulo bangla mān basda thiun. 6. Yo jagah ma eota sipahi sandai rāt ma pahra din thiyo. 7. Bilāyat jāna bhandā pahile ma Gurkhali rāmro bol thiyen. 8. Hamiharu jiāda garera dushman ko morcha ko khoj mān wahān jānda thiun. 9. Kye āfū yo sāmne ko ghar mān basda thiyau? 10. Jaba Cnpt. Hulse Sāhib wahān jāda thiye, ta jawānharu dherai khushi hunda thiye. 11. Karnal Sānib sandai jawānharu sita gurkhali kurā gardai thiye.

LESSON 19

THE FUTURE IMPERFECT TENSE.

Singniar

1. Ma gari rāhe ko hunlā ... I will be doing *or* I must be doing it.

2. T gari rahe ko holas ... Thou wilt be doing *or* Thou must be doing it.

3. Ū gari rahe ko holā ... He will be doing *or* He must be doing it.

Plural

1. Hamiharu gari rahe ka hounlā ... We must be doing it.
2. Timiharu gari rahe ka holau ... You must be doing it.
3. Ūniharu gari rahe ka holan ... They must be doing it.

Exercise—18

Translate into English. (consult the 'Key')

1. Gurūjī jwānharu lai Roman-Urdu parhaundāi holan 2. Ghoṛāharu maidān mān chardāi holan. 3. Naniharu maidān mān kheldāi holan. 4. Ū ghar baṭa āundāi holā. 5. Himmat Singh aile samman kām gardāi holā. 6. Jawānharu aile khānā khandāi holan. 7. Angrejī hawāi-jahaj Germonharu mathi gola bārī gardāi holan. 8. Allen Sahib le āfū lāi sandāi patra lekhdāi holan.

LESSON 20

THE PAST CONDITIONAL TENSE.

The Past Conditional Tense is formed by using the Present Participle as the main Verb. Sometimes the word 'Agar' is used in the beginning of a sentence. (very seldom)

eg. (1) If you had written to me, I would havd answered you...Āphule malai lekhe ko bhaye ma jawāb dine thiyen,

(2) If you had come, I would have given him a letter... Timi āyeko bhaye ma uslai chiṭṭhi dine thiyen.

Exercise—19

Translate into English. (Consult the 'Key')

1. Usle dushman ko patā chal paye ko bhaye khabar jarur dine thiyo. 2. Ek ghanṭā pahile hamro jawān yahān hun thiye tā bhusak kai hoi jān thiye. 3. Hami dui baje na hinṛe ko bhaye belā mān pugne thiyenau. 4. Kholā mān pānī hun-thiyo tā dherai dukh hun-thiyo. 5. Agar āphū Gurkhali bolna jānda thiyau tā ḍherai sajilo hun-thiyo. 6. Ū yo kuā ko pānī khān-thiyo tā mari jān-thiyo. 7. Dushman yahān dekhi dekhai din-thiyo tā hami khabar paṭhai din thiyeun. 8. Āja pāni na paṛ thiyo tā hami jraur Mussoorie jān-thiyeun.

LESSON 21

ADJECTIVES.

Some Useful Adjectives.

Aged	... Buṛho	Heavy	... Garung
Blind	.. Andhā	Low	... Hocho
Bad	... Na-rāmro	Long	... Lāmo
Broad	... Chauṛā, thulo	Better	.. Bhanda, rāmro
Cheap	... Sasto	Bigger	... Bhanda-thulo
Clean	... Sāf	Smaller	... Bhanda-sano
Deep	... Gahiro	Light	... Halungo, halukā
Dirty	... Mailo	Lame	... Langro
Dear,(expensive)	...Mahngo	New	... Nayā
Difficult	... Kaṭhin, sāro	Old,(for things)	...Purāno
Deaf	... Bahiro	Soft	... Kamalo
Dumb	... Gonga	Short	.. Chhoto

Easy	... Sajilo	Thin	.. Pātlo
Fat	... Moṭo	Thick	... Bāklo
Good	... Rāmro	Weak	.... Kamjor
High	... Algo, Aglo	Worse	... Bhaṇda
Hard	... Sāro		-naramro.

Bhaṇdā = than. (In Comparison)

1.	Good ..	Better ...	Best
	Rāmro ...	Khub-rāmro ...	Sab bhaṇdā ramro
2.	High ...	Higher ...	Highest
	Ūṇcho ...	Bhaṇdā-ūṇcho...	Sab bhaṇdā ūṇcho
3.	Small ...	Smaller ...	Smallest
	Sāno ...	Bhaṇdā-sāno ...	Sab bhaṇdā sāno

Useful Sentences.

1. How old is he? ... Ū kati barsa pugyo?
2. This is better *than* that ... Tyo bhaṇdā yo rāmro chha.
3. How deep is the river? ... Yo khola kati gahiro chha?
4. This is the best ... Yo sab bhaṇdā rāmro ho.
5. Delhi is bigger *than* Lucknow. ... Delhi Lucknow bhaṇdā thulo chha.
6. Where is the nearest Post Office? ... Sab bhanda najik ko ḍāk-ghar kahāṇ chhā?
7. This is the nearst Post Office. ... Yo sab bhanda najik ko ḍāk-ghar ho.
8. Ram is better *than* Sohan... Ram Sohan bhaṇdā rāmro chha.
9. Dehra Dun is colder *than* Lucknow. ... Dehra Dun Lucknow bhaṇdā ṭhanḍā chha.
10. Which is the easiest way to Mussoorie? ... Mussoorie mā jāne sab bhaṇdā sajilo bāta kun chha?

LESSON 22

COMPOUND VERBS.

1. Intensive Compound.

The list of Intensive Verbs used in Gurkhali.

(1) Mārnu—to strike, (shows Violence). eg. Khub-mārnu = to strike hard to some one.

(2) Linu—to take, (It expresses the idea of one's own gain or advantage). eg. Khāī-linu = to eat.

(3) Rakhnu—to keep, (It expresses the idea of information, retention and requirement). eg. lekhí-rakhaye = keep it ready.

(4) Chhoṛnu—to leave, (It gives the idea of reference) eg. Rakhī-chhoṛnu = to keep it for an unlimited period.

(5) Paṛhnu—to read, eg. Parhi-hāla = Read it now.

(6) Ānu or āunu—to come, (It expresses the idea of having been) eg. Laī-āunu=to bring along.

(7) Nikālnu—to take out by force. eg. Nikāla=Take it out, [turn him out].

[8] Dinu –to give, [It expresses doing something for some one else] eg. Lekhi-deū = write it, Dīdeū = give it.

Exercise—20

Translate into English. (Consult the 'Key')

1. Yo chakku uṭhāi leu. 2. Sabai dawāi khāi leu. 3. Āfno kām mā lāgi jāu. 4. Chhiṭo khabar gari deu. 5. Pankhā kholi deu.

Exercise—21

Translate into Gurkhali. (Consult the 'Key')

1. I shall put your book on the table. 2. John wrote a letter for me. 3. He threw a book on the ground. 4. He has killed his enemy. 5. Colonel Sahib will explain your duties tomorrow. 6. Change these clothes at once. 7. The boy fell down from the horse. 8. They spoke out in the meeting.

LESSON 23

2. Potential Compound

Saknu = to be able

I am able to go	... Ma jan sak-chhu.
He is able to see it	... Usle dekhna sak-chha
He could write	... Usle lekhi sakiyo.
He is able to go	... Ū jai sak-chha.

Exercise—22

Translate into English. (Consult the 'Key')

1. Ū kasrat gari sak-chha. 2. Yo manchhe pahāṛ ko ṭuppā mā pugnu sak-chha. 3. Timi āram gari sak-chhau. 4. Ū sipāhī pānī mā pauri sak-chha. 5. Ram Lal āba kuchh khāi sak-chha.

Exercise—23

Translate into Gurkhali. (Consult the 'Key')

1. I can speak the Gurkhali language. 2. The boy can not read this book. 3. My brother could not come to-day. 4. When will they be able to go to the hospital? 5. He will not be able to catch the train. 6. Could you recognise me? 7. Can you show me the way to the Gurkha lines? 8. Can you speak English well? 9. How many can swim across this stream? 10. Can you do this work for me now?

LESSON 24

3. Completive Compound.

Bhiyaunu = to have finished, to be done.

I have finished my food ... Maile āfno khāna khāi liyān.

I have finished ... Maile khāi bhiyayen.

He has already seen it ... Usle dekhi sake ko chha.

Exercise—24

Translate into English. (Consult the 'Key')

1. Maile āfno kām gari bhiyānyen. 2. Hamile uslāi kati khep bhani sakyeūn. 3. Usle yo khel lai dekhi bhiyāyo. 4. Timile uslāi sabai bāt samjhāi halye ka chhau. 5. Manchhe-haru ramrai ghar pugi gae.

Exercise—25

Translate into Gurkhali. (Consult the 'Key')

1. The men had finished eating. 2. They have not finished their work. 3. Have you finished your Parade? 4. We will finish our food at 6, o'clock. 5. Have you finished your lesson ?

LESSON 25

4. The Relative and Correlative.

	Relative		*Correlative*	
1.	Jo	... (who, which, whoever).	Tyo	... (he, that same)
2.	Jasko	... Whose	Usko	... His
3.	Jaba	... When	Taba	... Then
4.	Jasto	... As	Usto	... So
5.	Jati	... As much as	Uti	... So much
6.	Jahān	... Where	Wahān	... There
7.	Jatāsukai	... Wherever	Uthai	... There
8.	Jadapi	... Although	Taba pomi	... Yet
9.	Jab samma	.. As long as	Tab samma	.. So long
10.	Jahān tak (samma)	... As far as	Wahān tak (samma)	... Upto that place

eg. If he had played, then we would not have been defeated ...Ū khelthyo, ta hami hārne thiyenau.

When he came then I went ... Jaba Ū āyo taba ma gayen.

LESSON 26

5. Desiderative Compound.

I want to go ... Ma janu māngchhu.
He wants to see it ... Usle herna māngchha.
I want to go to the station.. Ma *station* ma jānu māngchhu.
I want to write ... Ma lekhnu māngchhu.
I wish to go to the line ... Ma *line* mān jānu māngchhu.
I wish to play ... Ma khelnu māngchhu.

Exercise—26

Translate into English. (Consult the 'Key')

1. Hami dushman lāi jitnu māngchhun. 2. Hami shahr lāi barbād garnu māngchhun. 3. Ma āfu sita ijājat linu māngchhu. 4. Padam Singh bajār jānu māngchha. 5. Ū *hockey* khelnu māngchha.

Exercise—27

Translate into Gurkhali (Consult the 'Key')

1. I wish to see them. 2. I wish to learn the language of Nepal. 3. These Gurkhas wants to fight the Japs. 4. Do you wish to read this book? 5. My elder brother wishes to go to Delhi.

LESSON 27

6. Habitual Compound.

He is in the habit of going to bazar. ... Usle bajār jāne bāni chha
He used to go to the bazar... Ū bajār jānthiyo.

I used to write a long letter... Mā lāmo chiṭṭhī lekhthen.
They used to play in the evening. ... Uniharu belukā khel the.

Singular

1. Ma gar-thiyen ... I used to do.
2. Timi gar-thiyau ... You used to do
3. Ū gar-thiyo ... He used to do.

Plural

1. Hamiharu gar-thiyon ... We used to do.
2. Timiharu gar-thiyau ... You used to do.
3. Uniharu gar-thiye ... They used to do.

Exercise—28

Translate into English. (consult the 'Key')

1. Hami har sandhai usko ghar ma janthiyon. 2. Ma janthiyen. 3. Usle herthiyo Har hafta hami England ma patra lehh thiyon. 5. Ū ghar mā basthiyo. 6. Sārā din uniharu bāt gar-thiye. 7. Uniharu dui ghanṭā khelthiye.

Exercise—29

Translate into Gurkhali (consult the 'Key')

1. He used to write a letter to England every week. 2. They used to come to the Office at 10, o'clock. 3. We used to play tennis every evening at 5. 4. John used to work the whole day. 5. Boy's used to sleep in the tents.

LESSON 28

7. Impending *or* Imminent Action.

He is about to go ... { Ū jāne wālā chha. / Ū jāne lāi taiyār chha.

I am *about** to go ... Ma jānewālā thiyen̲.

N.B. *about is used here for 'uncertainty.'

Exercise—30

Translate into English. (Consult the 'Key')

1. Rel gāṛī *Station* ma āunewālā chha. 2. Ū bajār jāna lai taiyār chha. 3. Tej Bahadur aspatāl jānewālā chha. 4. Bālak sunta lai taiyār chha. 5. Mero ristedār yahān̲ āune-wālā chha.

Exercise—31

Translate into Gurkhali (consult the 'Key')

1. My father is about to come here. 2. The child is about to sleep. 3. He is about to write a long letter to England. 4. They are about to attack the enemy. 5. They were about to start now.

MISCELLANEOUS EXERCISES.

Mixed Exercise—32

(On different Tenses)

Translate into English. (Consult the 'Key')

1. Ma jan̲dai chhu. 2. Ū chāhos ta yahān̲ āos. 3. Capt. Sahib Gurkhali sikhi rahe ka chhau. 4. Malāi alikati dūdh deu. 5. Samāchār patra liyau. 6. Aj sān̲j ma āu. 7. Timro *boot* sāf gara. 8. Timro *coat* ma burus gara. 9. Pustak mej mān̲thi chha. 10. Usko lagi thama.

Mixed Exercise—33

(On different Tenses)

Translate into Gurkhali. (Consult the 'Key')

1. The book is on the table. 2. We will go to C. O. at 7, o'clock. 3. I shall send the books tomorrow. 4. He does not go to the lines every day. 5. May we go to the station? 6. It is raining, don't go to Mussoorie. 7. Will you have tea? 8. Go to the bazar and bring these things. 9. Fold up the clothes and put them away. 10. He is in the act of seeing it.

Mixed Exercise—34

(On different Tenses)

Translate into English. (Consult the 'Key')

1. Ū hāmra ghar dekhi āye. 2. Agar mānchhe yahān̲ basun ta ma sab bandobast garun̲. 3. Ū taiyār hos ta ma uslāi khāna mā bulāun̲. 4. Yahān̲ basyeko kati din bhayo. 5. Ma āfo ko parcel paṭhai rahe chhu. 6. Usle herdai thiyo. 7. Maile uslai boldai gare ko sune. 8. Kye āfū yo sāmne ko ghar mān̲ basda thiyau. 9. Ū ghar baṭa aun̲dāi hola. 10. Timi āyeko bhaye ma uslai chiṭṭhi dine thiyen̲.

Mixed Exercise—35

(On different Tenses)

Translate into Gurkhali. (Consult the 'Key')

1. Has he brought an answer? 2. Has the tailor come? 3. We had written a letter. 4. They had eaten their food. 5. If you had written to me, I would have answered you. 6. Dehra Dun is colder than Lucknow.

7. This is the best book. 8. I shall put your book on the table. 9. I can speak the Gurkhali language. 10. He has already seen it.

LESSON 29

8. Compulsive Compounds—(Expressing requirement, obligation, duty and fortune etc.)—are formed by prefixing the Infinitive to any of the following words:- paṛyo, chāhin chha, chha etc.

Useful Short Sentences.

1. I must go ... Malai jānu chha. (shows necessity)
2. I had to go ... Malai jānu paṛyo (shows strong compulsive).
3. I have to go ... Malai jānu par chha. (Necessity)
4. I will have to go .. Malai jānai par chha.
5. He ought to go ... Usle jānai parthiyo. (obligation)
6. I ought to have gone ... Malai jānu chāhin thiyo *or* (paṛne thiyo).
7. They ought to have written a letter ... Uniharulai chiṭṭhi lekhnu chāhin thiyo *or* (paṛne thiyo).

Exercise—36

(On *ought* and *ought to have*)

Translate into English. (Consult the 'Key')

1. Hamilai khub kām garnu chāhin thiyo. 2. Unilai āfno sāmān khabardāri le rākhnu chāhin thiyo. 3. Jīt Singh lai sajā dinu chāhin thiyo. 4. Uslai āfnu *duty* garnu chāhin

thiyo. 5. Havaldarlai nau baje pachhī line ma jānu chāhinna thiyo. 6. Hamilai ṭhik ṭhik pata lāunu paṛne thiyo. 7. Bahadur Singh lai bijjoi rahnu chāhin thiyo. 8. Usle khānā-pina ko ṭhik bandobast garnu paṛne thiyo. 9. Male usko patra ko uttar dinu paṛne thiyo. 10. Jawānharule saṇgin-le hamlā garnu paṛne thiyo.

Exercise—37

(on *have to* and *will have to* and *had to*)

Translate into English. (Consult the 'Key')

1. Malāi jaldi isṭeshan pugnu chha. 2. Jawanharu lai bihāna uṭhnu chhā. 3. Hamilai bandūk sāf garnu chha. 4. Timile dushman lai harāunu chha. 5. Ram Singh lai '*operation*' garāunu chha. 6. Malāi dushman sita laṛnai paṛlā 7. Jawanharulai āfno kām khatam garnai paṛlā. 8. Havaldarlai sārā hisāb dinai paṛlā. 9. Uslai imtihān *pass* garnai paṛlā. 10. Āj sablai bandūk sāf garnai paṛlā. 11. Malai ek mahina ko chhuṭṭī linu paṛyo. 12. Mohan Lal nadi pār garnu paṛyo. 13. Ganga Singh lai sahar baṭa bhāgnu paṛyo. 14. Gopal lai āfno ghar khālī garnu paṛyo. 15. Sohan lai diwāl nāṇgnu paṛyo.

Exercise--38

Translate into Gurkhali. (Consult the 'Key')

1. I must do it now. 2. He ought to come to the class. 3. You should fight with all your might. 4. They should come here at 2 p. m. 5. You must obey the order. 6. John ought to work well. 7. I ought to have written a letter. 8. You ought to have gone there yesterday.

9. I ought not to have done this work. 10. She ought to have stayed there for a week. 11. He has to see it 12. I will have to go to the Station. 13. He will have to see it. 14. He had to go to the lines. 15. I had to write a letter.

LESSON 30

9. Inceptive Compound.

To begin = lāgnu.

To begin, when used with a noun, it is translated by 'shuru garnu' *or* shuru hunu.

Useful Sentences.

1. He began to see ... Usle dekhna lagyo.
2. I began the work ... Male kām shuru garen.
3. The game began ... Khel shuru bhayo.
4. I began to go ... Ma janu thalen.
5. He began to see it ... Usle hernu thālio.

Exercise—39

Translate into English. (Consult the 'Key')

1. Bāgh ghurrnā lágyo. 2. Ū bajār jāna lāgyo. 3. Bahadur Singh roṭī khāna lāgyo. 4. Ū kām garna lāgyo. 5. Ma dui baje bāṭa aphna pāṭh paṛhna lāgyen.

LESSON 31

10. Permissive Compound.

To let, to allow = Dinu.

1. I gave him ... Maile uslai diyen.

2. I let him go ... Maile uslai janu diyen.
3. He let him see it ... Usle uslai hernu diyo.

Exercise—40

Translate into English. (consult the 'Key')

1. Maile uslāi kamra bāṭa janu diyen. 2. Unle John lāi Hindustani sikhna diye. 3. Hamile uslai *Football* khelna diyeu. 4. Timile uslāi yo pustak paṛhna diyeu. 5. Maile uslāi jāna diyan kinaki Ū bimār thiye.

LESSON 32

11. Acquisitive Compound

To be allowed
or
To find. = Pāunu.

1. I found a pen ... Maile eota kalam payen.
2. I was not allowed to go home ... Ma ghar jānu pāi na.
3. I was not allowed to go ... Ma jāna sakin-na.
4. He was not allowed to see it ... Usle hernu payena.

LESSON 33

12. To receive / To find / To get / To meet } = MILNU.

The Subject takes 'lāi' and the verb agrees with the object in gender and number.

1. How much salary he gets ? or What is his salary ? = Uslai kati tankha mil-chha.

Exercise – 41

Translate into English. (Consult the 'Key')

1. Timilai dui hafta ko chhuṭṭi millā. 2. Uslai kati rupia mil-chha. 3*Ū āimāile kati tankha paunchhe. 4. Ū āimāi lāi kati tankha mil-chha. 5. Āja ū malāi milyo. 6*Ma āja ū sang milyen. 7.*Hamro lagi pānī liāu.

N.B. *No 'lāi' is used in No. 3, 6 and 7, Sentences.

LESSON 34

13. Infinitive Used as a Noun.

To go = Jānu.

To see it = Dekhnu, heṛnu.

Exercise—42

Translate into English. (Consult the 'Key')

1. Khānā har koi ko lāgi jaruri chha. 2. Kasai ko dil dukhaunu kharāb ho. 3. Imtihān ko lāgi koshish garnu jaruri chha. 4. Sāncho bolnu rāmro gun ho, 5. Samai lāi khāli jāna dinu narāmro ādat ho.

LESSON 35

14. I heard him Speaking = Maile uslai boldai gare ko sune.

He saw him doing it = Usle uslai gardai gare ko dekhyo.

Exercise—43

Translate into English. (Consult the 'Key')

1. Maile uslāi sute ko dekhen. 2. Usle uslāi dugre ko dekhyo. 3. Maile uniharulāi bāt gare ko sune. 4. Tej Bahadur le uslai raksi khaye ko dekhyo. 5. Maile ūlāi patra lekhe ko dekhen.

Exercise—44

Translate into Gurkhali. (Consult the 'Key')

1. We saw him writing a letter. 2. They heard him speaking in the church. 3. I saw him going to the bazar in the evening. 4. Did you see them playing football. 5. John saw Mrs. Jones going to the dance.

LESSON 36

15. It is necessary for him to see it ... Usle herna jaruri chha.

Exercise—45

Translate into English. (Consult the 'Key')

1. Uslai jānu chāhin chha. 2. Uslai pachha hatnu chāhin chha. 3. Uslai khelnu chāhin chha. 4. Jīt Singh lai āunu chāhin chha. 5. John Sāhib lai imtihān dinu chāhin-chha.

Exercise—46

Translate into Gurkhali (consult the 'Key')

1. It is necessary for you to go to the station today.

2. It is necessary for them to write a long letter. 3. It is necessary for John to come to the Office. 4. It is necessary for me to see Colonel Sāhib. 5. It is necessary for you to sleep at least 2 hours.

LESSON 37

16. I tried to go = Maile janu lai koshish gare<u>n</u>.

He tried to see it = Usle herna koshish garyo.

Exercise—47

Translate into English. (Consult the 'Key')

1. Usle karnel sāhib lai dekhnu koshish garyo, tara dekhin sakena. 2. Unle hāmro manchhe laijānu koshish garye. 3. Maile 'rifle' *fire* garna koshish gare<u>n</u>. 4. Hamile dushmanlāi khojna koshish garyeū<u>n</u>. 5. Maile *Gurkhali* bolna koshish garye<u>n</u>.

LESSON 38

17. Recapitulation of an Intransitive Verb.

Root

1. Go ... Jāu.
2. Please go .. Jānu hos.
3. Will you please go? ... Jānu hos.
4. Having gone ... Gayera.
5. I am in the act of going ... Ma jandai chha.

6. I have already gone ... Ma gayen.
7. If I should go he would go .. Ma gayan bhane ū jān chha.
8. I will go ... Ma jāne chhu.
9. I am able to go ... Ma jāna sak-chhu.

Present Participle.

10. I am going ... Ma jandai chhu.
11. I was going ... Ma jandai thiyen.
12. If I had gone he would not have gone. ... Ma jando hun ta ū jāne thiyena.
13. I must be going ... Ma jāndai hun chhu.
14. I keep on going ... Ma hindai rahan chhu.
15. I kept on going ... Ma jāndai gāren.
16. I go on writing ... Ma lekhdai jān-chhu.
17. I heard him speaking ... Maile uslai boldai gare ko sune.

Past Participle

18. I went ... Ma gayen.
19. I have gone ... Ma gaye ko thiyen.
20. I had gone .. Ma gaye ko thiyen.
21. I must have gone ... Ma gayen ko hola.
22. I used to go ... Ma jan then.
23. Did you do as I told you? ... Jasto bhane then ustai gareū.
24. (a) To be seen .. (a) Dekhinu.
    (b) He will be seen ...(b) Uslai dekhine chha.
    (c) He is being seen ...(c) Uslai dekhindai chha.
    (d) He has been seen ...(d) Uslai dekhiye ko chha
    (e) He was seen ...(e) Uslai dekhīyo.
    (f) He had been seen ...(f) Uslai dekhiye ko thiyo

25. I caused (him) to sleep ... Maile (uslai) sutānye.

Infinitive

26. I want to go ... Ma jānu māngchhu.
27. I will have to go ... Malai jānai paṛchha.
28. I have to go ... Ma jānu chha.
29. I had to go ... Malai jānu paryo.
30. I ought to go ... Malai jānu parchha.
31. I ought to have gone ... Malai jānu paṛne thiyo.

Inflected Infinitive

32. I went to see him ... Ma uslai hernu gāyen.
33. I began to go .. Ma jānu thālen.
34. I am about to go { Ma jāne-wālā chhu.
Ma jāne-lai taiyar chhu.
35. I let him go ... Maile (uslai) jānā diyen.
36. I tried to go ... Ma janu koshish gāren.
37. I did not manage to go *or* I was not allowed to go. } = Ma jāna sakin-na.

Extra Forms

38. I need (*or* require) one book. ... Malai ek pustak chāhin chha.
39. It is necessary for him to see. ... Usle hernu jaruri chha.
40. Go away (Emphatic) ... Jai—jāu.

IMPORTANT TOPICS for EVERY—DAY USE.

LESSON 39

Time.

Evening	... Sānjh, beluka.
Morning	... Bihān, bhiyāna.
Now	Aile
Tomorrow	... Bholi
Last week	... Gayeko hafta.
Come tomorrow	... Bholī āu.
Come this evening	... Āju belukā āu.
Come after four	... Chār baji bād āu.
Come before six	... Chha baji bhandā aghī āu.
Yesterday	... Hijo.
Time	... Belā, baja.
Today	... Āju, Āj.
Day before yesterday	... Asti.
Come at 2, o'clock	... Dui baje ān.
Go there at 4, p. m.	... 4 baje belukā wahān jāu.
Go there at 10, a. m.	... 10 baje bihānā wahan jāu.
What is the time?	... Kati bajyo *or* kati baji?
Remind me tomorrow	... Bholi malai samjhāunu.
It is 2, o'clock	... Dui baji
It is 2:15	... Sawā dui baji.
It is 2:30	... Dhāī baji.

It is 1:45	... Paune dui baji.
Five minutes past 2	... Dui bajiera panch minaṭ.
5 to two	... Dui bajnu ma 5 minaṭ.

LESSON 40

Useful Sentences on Daily Parade.

A short step	... Chhoṭo qadam.
A long step	... Lamo qadam.
A little to the right	... Alīk dāhine tira.
A little to the left	... Alīk bāyān tira.
Are you tired?	... Timi thakyeau.
At what time the parade will be dismissed.	... Kati baje *parade dismiss* hun chha.
At what time parade will be started.	... Parade kati baje shuru hun chha?
A soldier should always salute an officer.	... Sipahi le afsar lai sandai *salute* garnu chāhin chha.
Be silent	... Chup lag, chup chap legera bas.
Be careful	... Hoshiyār ho.
Back a little	... Alīk pachhi.
Blow your whistle	... Siṭī baja.
Bring the chest forward	... Chhatī aghi gara. (gar).
Close up	... *Close* gar, (mili jāu).
Come behind me	... Mero pachhī āunu.
Come one step forward	... Ek qadam agi āu.
Carry (your) right foot 8 inches to the right.	... Dahine khuṭṭa 8 inch dahine tira laijāu.
Don't run	... Na dauṛa.

Don't hold the breath	... Sāns na rok.
Don't forget	... Na bhūl.
Don't move	... Na hilā, (Na hil).
Don't speak in the line	... *Line* ma na bolā. (*Line* ma na bol.)
Don't look down, lookto your front.	... Tala na hera *or* her, sāmne hera *or* her.
Don't lean forward	... Aghi na jhuk.
Don't swing your hands	... Hāth na hilāu.
Don't bend the left knee	... Bāyān ghunra na jhukāu.
Don't spit here and there	... Yahān wahān na thuk.
Do some brain exercise after the parade.	... *Parade* ko akheri ma alīk magaj barhaune ko kasrat garnu.
Draw your stomach in	... Peṭ bhitra gar.
Drop your hands	... Hāth tala jhar.
Don't put your finger on the trigger.	... Aunla tigger ma na rakh.
Fall in for parade	... *Parade* ko lāgi *fall* in gara.
Form four line	... Chār *line* banāu.
Form a line	... Line banāu.
Get up at once	... Ek dam uṭhā, (uṭh).
Go away	... Jai jā.
Go straight there	... Wahān sidha jau.
Get in step with the drum	... Dhol ko sang ma qadam mila.
Hold the rifle tight	... Raifal mazbūt sāth pakṛa.
Hurry up and put down your rifle.	... Raifal chhito rakh.
He never used to come late	.. Ū dhilo kaile pani aundaina thiyo.
He refused to do whatever he was ordered (to do)	.. Usle bhanyeko jasto manena.

Have one foot distance from the person in front of you.	... Afno aghi ko manchhe dekhi ek foot ko fāsla rakha.
I am late	... Malai dhilo bhayo.
It is too late	... Dherai aber bhayo.
In the front line	... Aghi *line* ma.
In the rear line	... Pachhi *line* ma.
Keep alert	... Chankho sita bas.
Keep back	... Pichharī bas.
Keep elbows close to your sides.	... Kuhina pahlu sanga milāu.
Keep your heels in line and together.	... Eṛī ek sāth milaera ek *line* ma rakha.
Keep your hands close to the body.	... Hāth badan sanga milāu.
Keep (your) body straight	... Badan sidhā rakha.
Keep your shoulders back	... Timi kūm pachhī gara, *or*(gar)
Keep your feet apart	... Khuttā alag gar.
Keep your feet 12 inches apart.	... Khuttā barāh *inch* ko fasla ma rakha.
Keep your hands straight	... Hāth sidha rakha.
Look to your front	... Sāmne hera *or* her or sidhā her.
Look	... Herai.
Look at me	... Malai her.
Look up	... Mathi hera *or* (her).
Lie down on the ground	... Jamin ma leṭi jāu *or* (suti jāu).
Look to the distance of 300 yards.	... Tīn sau gaj aghi hera.
Lean more forward	... Ajai aghi jhuka.
Move more to the left hand	... Ajhai bayān tira sar.
Move one step back	... Ek qadam pachhi jāu.

One step forward ... Ek qadam agi (āu).
One step back ... Ek qadam pachhi (iāu).
Open your eyes ... Ankha kholā (khol).
Pick up your rifle ... Timro raifal tip.
Put your hand up .. Hāth uṭhā.
Put your shoulders back ... Chhātī khol.
Rear rank come in front ... Pichhāṛī ko manchhe-haru agharī āunu.
Raise your head ... Sir sidhā gara *or* (gar).
Shut up ... Chup chāp lagera bas.
Stand straight ... Sidhā kharā ho.
Stand with your heels together. ... Eṛī milāera kharā ho.
Show him how to do it ... Uslai kasari garnu parne ho dekha.
Step together ... Qadam milāu.
Step by step ... Qadam qadam ma.
Step out ... Bahira niska.
Take two steps ... Dui qadam phailāu.
Turn together ... Ek sang ghuma.
To the left hand ... Bayān *or* bāen tira.
To the right hand ... Dahine tira.
Turn that way ... Uta tira ghum.
There is too much distance... Bahut fāsla bho.
Walk straight ... Sojho hinṛ.
Was Jit Singh present on parade today? ... Kye Jīt Singh āja *parade* ma hājir thiyo?
What do you call this in Gurkhali? ... Eslai Gurkhali ma kye bhanchha?
What has happened ? / What is the matter ? ... Ke bhayo ? / Ke bāt chhā ?
What is the reason of this? ... Yesko ke kāran chha ?

What do you want? ... Kye māngchhau?
Why did you not come? ... Timi kina āyenāu?
Where were you this morning? ... Āja bihānā timi kahān thiyeū?

LESSON 41

Rifle Drill

Don't be late ... Dhilo na garnu.
He is active ... Furti manchhe chha.
Hold the rifle tightly with the right hand. ... Dāhine hāth le raifal jor sanga pakṛā.
Hold the rifle more up-right .. Raifal ajai sidha umbho pakṛa.
How many cartridges are there in your pouch? ... Timro ponch ma kati kārtus chha?
Keep the bullets always dry . Golīharu sandāi sukha rakha.
Keep the back-sight up ... *Back-sight* sidhā rākha.
Keep (your) right arm against the butt. ... Dāhine pakhura *butt* sanga lagāi rakha.
Look at the target ... *Target* ma hera.
Listen to me ... Mero bāt sun.
My rifle was lying on the ground. ... Mero raifal bhuin ma thiyo.
Rifle is loaded ... Raifal bhare ko chha.
Send another man ... Arko manchhe lai paṭhai dinu.
Step out ... Qadam baṛhāu.
They had twenty rifles ... Uniharu sanga bis raifal thiyo.
Take care, the rifle is loaded... Hoshiyār, raifal bhare ko chha.
Take out the cartridges ... Kartūs nikāla.

LESSON 42

Camp

Clean the ground in the camp. ...	Camp bhitra zamīn sāf gara.
Does this (Kachha) road goes to the camping ground. ..	Yo (kachha) bāṭo camp mā jānchha.
Don't throw dirty water here and there in the camp. ...	Camp ma yahān wahān mailo pānī na phenka.
How far is the camp from here? ...	Paṛāo yahān dekhi kati dūr chha?
No one should cook food in the camp. ...	Camp bhitra khānā pakāunu chahinna.
Pitch a tent here ...	Yahān chholdārī lagau.
Strike a tent ...	Chholdārī khola.
These tent-ropes should be tightened. ...	Yo tambu doriharu kasnu chahin chha.
Where is the camp? ...	Camp kahan chha?
Whose is this large tent ...	Yo ṭhulo chholdārī kasko ho?

LESSON 43

(a) Pay

Do you get pay weekly *or* monthly? ...	Timi talab haftawār yā mahāwārī paun chhau?
Do you get any free allowance? ...	Timilai koi bhatta mil chha?
What is your pay? ...	Timro talab kati chha?
What pay does a soldier get? ...	Sipahi lai mahina pichhe kati talab mil chha?

(b) Leave

Absenting himself without leave.	... Chhuṭṭi manjurī binā gair-hāzir hunu.
Pretending to be sick	... Bimārī ko bahānā garnu.
The Corporal Himmat Siṅgh has gone on leave.	... Naik Himmat Singh chhuṭṭi ma gayo.

LESSON 44

Education

Ask various kinds of questions.	.. Bhinnai bhinnai khal ko sawal sodhnu.
Come to the School •	... School mā āu.
Can you read and write?	... Timi lekhnu, paṛhnu sak-chha?
How many men were in the class?	... Class ma kati jana thiyo?
How many pupil are in your class?	... Timro class ma kati chela chhan?
I want you to do this	... Yo kām timile nain garyeko māngchhu.
Let him do it himself	... Ū aphai le-garos.
This man ins't trying to learn Roman-Urdu.	... Yo manchhe Roman Urdu sikhnu koshish gardaina.
Think before you give an answer.	... Jawāb dinu bhanda aghari sochnu.
Whose turn is it?	... Kasko palo ho chha?
Where is Jit Bahudar?	... Jīt Bahudar khoi?
When do you begin your examination?	.. Timro imtihān kaile shuru hunchha?

Which is the way to the School?	... School ko bāṭo kun ho?
What sort of book is this?	... Yo kasto kitāb ho?

LESSON 45

Military Questions (Interrogative Sentences).

How many clothes are there?	... Wahāṉ katiwatā lugā-fātā chhan?
How far is your house?	... Timro ghar kati taṛo chha?
How many children have you?	.. Timra katiwata nānīharu chhan?
How far is the next station where there is water?	.. Arka pānī milne jagah kati tāṛo chha?
How long will it take to get to the station?	... Station pugnu kati *time* lāg chha?
How far is your city?	... Timro shahr kati tāṛo chha?
How far is your village from here?	... Timro gāoṉ yahāṉ dekhi kati taṛo chha?
How is your helth?	... Timro swāstha (mijāj) kasto chha?
How shall I go there?	... Ma wahāṉ kasari jauṉ?
How many brothers have you in the Army?	... Fauj ma timro kati jānā dāju-bhai chha?
How far is it from the lines?	... *Line* dekhi kati tāro chha?
How deep is the river?	... Kholā kati gahiro chha?
How will you do it?	... Timile kasari garchhaū?
How many petrols are there in your regiment?	... Timro palṭan ma kati *petrol* chha?

How many years service have you? ... Timro naukri kati sāl bhayo ?

How many times are you on duty in a month? ... Mahina ma kati khep timro *duty* āunchha?

How far is the 3rd. Gurkha... centre? ... Yahān dekhi *3rd. Gurkha centre* kati taro chha?

How many cartridges are there in your pouch? ... Timro *pouch* ma kati kārtus chha?

How many men did you count? ... Kati manchhe ganyau?

How long has your hospital .. been in this city? .. Timro aspatāl kaile dekhi yo shahr mā chha?

How long have you been living in the lines? .... Line ma basyeko kati din bhoyo?

How many Subedars are there in each army? ... Har ek fauj mā kati subedār chha?

How far is 2nd. Gurkha centre from here? ... 2nd Gurkha centre yahān dekhi kati tāro chha?

How much do we owe you .. (Timro) kati tirne ho?

Who will go with me to Calcutta? ... Ma sanga *Calcutta* ko jān chha?

Who told you this? ... Yo bāt kasle timi lai bhanyo?

Who is incharge of the *Mess*? ... *Mess* kasko zimma ma chha?

Who is the C. O. of your army? ... Timro palṭan ko C. O. ko chhau?

Who is the owner of this house? ... Yo ghar ko mālik ko ho?

Who is there? ... Tinhān ko chha?

Who is he? ... Tyo ko ho?

Who are those people?	... Ti mānisharu ko hun?
Who enlisted him?	... Uslāi kasle bhartī garyo?
Who is the Commander of this company?	.. Yo *company* ko kamanḍar ko chha?
Who will stop them?	... Ūniharu lāi kasle roklā?
What is the date today?	.. Āju kun tārik ho?
What animal is that?	... Tyo jantu kye ho?
What is he doing?	... Ū (or tyo) yanhān ke gardai chha?
What is the time?	... Kati bajyo?
What do you say?	... Timro bhạnnu ke chha? *or* Timi ke bhan chhāu?
What is your work?	... Timi kye kām gar-chhāu?
What is the chief food of a soldier?	... Sipahi ko khās chīz khāne ko kye (*or* ke) ho?
What is your regiment?	... Timi kun palṭan ma chhau?
What regiment is here?	... Yahān aile kun palṭan base ko chha?
What is the matter?	... Kye ho *or* kye bho?
What is the news today?	... Āja ke khabar chha?
What arms have you?	... Timro pās kun hathiyār chhan?
What is his rank?	... Usko padbi kye chha?
What time will the drill be over?	... Kati baje *parade* khatam huni bho?
When the Company comes, open the front door?	.. Jạba company āulā, sāmne ko dhokā kholnu?
When will you go?	... Timi kaile jān-chhau?
When did you get promotion?	... Timilai kaile taraqqi milyo?
When did you enrol (*or* enlist)?	... Timi kahile bhartī bhayeu?

When will the regiment march? ... Palṭan kaba hinṛ chha?

When was the army captured? ... Palṭan kaba qnabja bhaye ko thiyo?

When do you begin your examination? ... Timro imtihan kaile shuru hunchha?

When will you return? ... Timi kaile farkan chhaū?

When did you come? ... Timi kaile āyeū?

When will you get married? .. Timro bibāh (biha) kaile hunchha?

When did you get married? .. Timro bibāh (*or* biha) kaile bhayo?

Where is your residence? ... Timro ghar kanhān chha (*or* bho)?

Where did you hear this news? ... Yo khabar timile kanhān suneū?

Where is my servant? ... Mero nakur kanhān chha?

Where were you before? .. Timro aghi kahān thiyo?

Where is your unit now? ... Timro *unit* aile kahān chha?

Where are you going? ... Timi kanhān jāndai chhāū?

Where do you live? ... Timi kanhān bas chhāū?

Where is the *boiled rice*? ... Bhāt kahān chha?

Which is the way to 2nd. G. R. C. ... 2nd. G. R. C. ko bāṭo kun ho?

Which is the shortest way to the lines? ... Line ko sab bhanda chhoṭo bāṭo kun chha?

Why don't you keep clean? .. Timi kina safā basdai nāū?

Why do you go there? ... Timi wahān kina jānchhāū?

Why did you not come? ... Timi kina āyenāū?

Why did you dismiss him ... Timi le uslai kina nikāli diyau?

Why did you disobey the orders of your Officer?	... Timile āfnu afsar ko kina hukūm māne nāu?
Whom do you want to see?	... Timi kaslai bheṭnu māngchhau?

LESSON 46

Useful Military phrases.

A petrol will set out tomorrow.	... *Petrol* bholī jane bho.
Arrest them	... Uniharu lāi qaid gar.
Bring me a cup	Eota piyāla (batu ko) liāū.
Bring some sugar	... Alikatā chinī liāū.
Bring some milk	... Alikatā dūdh liāū.
Bring my shoes	... Mero juttā liāū.
Bring the newspaper	... Akhbār (khabar kagaj) liāū.
Bring an answer	... Jawāb liāū.
Clean this table	... Yo mej safā gara.
Call the tailor .	... Damai (Darzī) lai bulāū.
Come at 2: o'clock	... Dui baje āū.
Come in	... Bhitra āū.
Come here	... Yahān āū.
Come near	... Najīk āū.
Come soon	... Chhito āū.
Come back	. Farki āū.
Come to the school	... School ma āū.
Come this evening	.. Āju belukā āū.
Come tomorrow	... Bholī āū.
Come again	... Pheri āū.
Come alone	... Eklai āū.

Come before six	... Chha baji bhanda aghi āū.
Come after four	... Chār baji bād āū.
Don't come tomorrow	... Bholī na āū.
Don't forget	... Na bhula.
Don't bother me	... Dik na deū.
Don't go there	... Wahāṉ na jāū.
Don't wait	... Na parkha.
Don't you know	... Timi lai thāhā chhaina.
Don't make a noise	... Halla na gara.
Don't put it there	... Wahāṉ na rakha.
Don't do it in future	.. Aba esto na garnu.
Do you know him?	... Tainle uslai chin chhas?
Do as I tell you to do	... Jasto bhanchhu testai gar.
Go to the Post Office	... Dākghar jāū.
Go to the Doctor	... Dākṭar ko mā jāū.
Go to the Washerman	.. Dhobī ko mā jāū.
Go there	... Wahāṉ jāū.
Go there at 4: p. m.	... 4 baji beluka wahāṉ jāū.
Go there at 10: a. m.	... 10 baji bihānā wahāṉ jāū.
Go away from here	... Yahāṉ dekhi jāū.
Go to the Office	... Daftar mā jāū.
Give me a cup of tea	... Ek batu ko chahā deū.
Give it to me	.. Malai deū.
Give it to him	.. Uslai deū.
Give me some milk	... Malai alikatā dūdh deū.
Give him my compliments	... Uslai mero salām deū.
Make haste, (Hurry up)	... Chiṭṭo gara.
Make up one's mind	... Afno dil ma thāni linu.
Show it to me	... Malai dekhāū.
Show it to him	... Uslāi dekhāū.

Send it to him ... Usko mā pathai deu.

Send it before four o'clock .. Chār baji ko aghi pathāu.

LESSON 47

Enlisting the Recruits (or Admission of Recruits).

What is your name? .. Tapain ko shub nām ke ho *or* Timro nām kye ho?

What is your father's name? ... Timro Buba (or bābu) ko ke nām ho?

What is the name of your Village? ... Timro gaon ko ke nām ho?

How far is it? ... Ū yahān dekhin kati taro chha?

When did you come? ... Timi kaile yahān āunu bho?

Do you want to be enrolled? ... Timi bhartī hunu chāhin chhau?

Are you willing to be enrolled in our army? ... Hāmro palṭan ma bhartī hunu rājī chhas?

Are you consented to serve in the British army? .. Timi angrezī palṭan ma naukarī garnu rājī chhau?

What Caste are you? ... Timi kasma hunu hun chhau?

How old are you?
What is your age? } ... Timi katī barsā ko (bhayo) *or* chhau?

Whose son are you? ... Timi kasko chhora (ho) or hau?

What is your religion? ... Timro dharam kun ho?

Your Caste will not interfere in your Military service. ... Timro jati le fauj ko kām? ma koi hani ta pahunchne chhaina.

You will have to serve the Govt. for the duration of war. ...	Timlai laṛāi huinjel naukri garnu parla.
In what district is your village situated? ...	Timro gaon kun zilla ma chha?
How far is the railway station from your village? ...	Timro gaon rel ko *Station* dekhi kati taṛo chha?
How many days it will take you to reach your village ...	Gaon ma pugni kati din lag chha?
You will get very little salary in the beginning ...	Timi lai pahle thoṛai talab millā.
Where-ever the Govt. will send you, you will have to go there. ...	Timi lāi jahān sarkarle paṭhaula wahān jānu parlā.
When did you enlist? ...	Timi kaile bhartī bhayeu
How many brothers have you? ...	Timiharu kati bhāi chhau?
How many brothers are already serving in the Army?	Kati bhai palṭan ma bharti chhau?
In what regiment your brother is serving? ...	Timro daju bhai kun palṭan ma bharti chhau?
You should answer these things truthfully (or honestly). ...	Timile sānchi sānchi inhi kura ko jawāb deu.
Where was this man enlisted? ...	Yo manchhe kahān bhartī bho?
Who enlisted him? ...	Uslai kasle bharti garyo?
Is your father and mother alive (or living)? ...	Timro āmā-bābu jiundai chhan?

Do you have any land? ...	Timro koi jamin chha?
Do you like to be a soldier? ...	Timilai sipahi hunu ramro lāgchha?
Are you able to read and write? ..	Timi lekhnu paṛhnu sak-chhau?

LESSON 42

Ration

What provisions has he brought? ...	Usle kye kye khāne chīz liyaye ko chha?
What supplies can we get here? ...	Yahāṉ khāne chīz ke pahinchha?
What quantity of rations is issued to every soldier? ..	Harek sipahi lai kati ration mil-chha?
What time do you get rations daily? ..	Sandai *ration* timilai kati baje mil-chha?
Who gives the rations? ...	Ration kasle banṭdai chha?
What things do you get? ...	Timilai kye kye *jinis* mil-chha?
We get flour, rice, dal, ghee, patotoes, sugar, tea leaves, wood and meat. ...	Hamilai, aṭo, chāwal, dāl, gheu, ālū, chinī, chha pattī, lakṛī sikār mil-chha.
Do you get rations every-day? ...	Timilai roj roj *ration* mil-chha?
No, we get once a week ...	Nahīṉ hafta ma ek dafe mil-chha.
Do you have any complaint to make about rations? ...	Kye timile *ration* ko barā ma kei bhannu mangchhau?

How many times a week do you get meat?	... Sikār kati dafe (*or* palo) mil-chha ?
Do you get any extra money for species?	... Masalo ko paisa alag mil-chha?

LESSON 49

Talking to a Sube-dar

Subedār Sāhib come in	... Subedār Sāhib bhitra āunu hos.
Please sit down	... Basnu hos.
How are you?	... Rājī khushī chau?
You have come after a long time.	... Timi dherai din ma āunu bho.
How is your family?	... Nani-haru sabai jātinai chhan?
When did you come back from active service?	... Timi laṛāī dekhin kaile āunu bhayo (or bho)?
How is your sick child?	... Timro birānī nanī kasto chhan?
Thank you, he is alright	... Dannebad ! ū jātinai chha
How many months leave have you taken?	... Tapainle kati mahina ko chhuṭṭī linu bho?
I have taken 3 months leave.	... Maile tīn mahina ko chhuṭṭī liye ko chhu.
May I help you in any way?	... Ma tapain ko kasai tarah le gohar gari sak-chhu?
No, there is no need	... Ji nahīn, kei garnu pardai na.
Whenever, you are free, come again.	... Jaba timilai fursat hola taba āunu hos.

LESSON 50

Relations

English		*Gurkhali*
Step-father	...	Kakā babu, saute babu.
Father	...	Bābu.
Father's father	...	Baje.
Father's brother	..	Kanchoba.
Father's mother	...	Bajai.
Father's brother's wife	...	Kanchhiamā.
Father's sister's husband	..	Pusain.
Father-in-law	...	Sasura.
Father's sister	...	Phupu.
Father's brother's son	...	Daju.
Father's brother's daughter	...	Baini.
Mother	...	Āmāji.
Step-mother	...	Kanchhiama, sauteniāma.
Mother's father	..	Bāje.
Mother's mother	...	Bajai.
Mother's brother	...	Mamaji.
Mother's brother's wife	...	Maijūji.
Mother's sister's husband	...	Kanchhoba.
Mother's sister	...	Kanchhiama.
Mother-in-law	...	Sasūji.
Son	...	Chhora, putr.
Son-in-law	...	Jawāin.
Son's son	...	Nati.
Son's daughter	..	Natini.
Daughter	...	Chhorī.
Daughter-in-law	..	Bowāri, Bohārī.

Daughter's daughter	... Natini.
Daughter's son	... Nāti.
Brother	{ Elder brother ... Dāju. Younger brother ... Bhāī.
Brother's son	... Bhatījā.
Brother's daughter	... Bhatījī.
Brother's wife	... Bhaojū, Bowārī.
Sister	{ Elder sister ... Didijī. Younger sister ... Bainijī
Sister's son	... Bhānja.
Sister's daughter	... Bhānjī.
Sister's husband	... Bahnoī.
Wife's sister	. Sālī.
Wife's brother	... Sālā.
Husband's elder brother	... Jethājui.
Husband's elder brother's wife.	... Didijī.
Husband's younger brother	Nani.
Husband's younger brother's wife.	... Bahin.
Husband's sister's husband	... Nandebhai.
Husband's sister	... Nani.
Wife	... Suāsni, āimāi.
Husband	... Logane.
Relation	... Sainoparne.
People	.. Manchheharu.
Friend	... Sāthī.
Friendship	... Mīt, Sangī.

"THE KEY"

Exercise—1 (Page—6)

1. Give me a cup of tea. 2. Make haste. 3. Don't do it in future. 4. Don't put it there. 5. Don't make a noise. 6. Go to the Office. 7. Come to the School. 8. Bring the newspaper. 9. Come this evening. 10. Go away from here.

Exercise—2 (Page—6)

1. Chhe dekhin pahile āu. 2. Chār dekhin pachhi āu. 3. Khola tak jāu. 4. Topī baks māthi chha. 5. Station dekhi pārsal lāu. 6. Ū koṭhā ma chha, dhoka khola. 7. Es lāi bistārā mathi rākha. 8. Ek tāngā bolāu. 9. Darji lāi bolāu. 10. Yo jhiāl band gara.

Exercise—3 (Page—8)

1. Give me a knife and a fork. 2. Clean your boats. 3. Call the servant. 4. Put the bread and butter on the table. 5. Brush your coat. 6. Wash your clothes. 7. Go by Lorry. 8. Open the door. 9. Take cover. 10. March slowly.

Exercise—4 (Page—9)

1. Yahān pathāu. 2. Ek patrol pathāu. 3. Uniform lagāu. 4. Lugā khola. 5. Uni harulāi pakra. 6. Yo lārī ma sāmān bhara. 7. Bholi bihān sahr ma āu. 8. Bazar jāu. 9. Eta āu. 10. Eta aija, (āu)

Exercise—5. (Page—12)

1. What is the name of this city? 2. What were you doing before enlisting? 3. When I was in the bazar? 4. How far is the camp from here? 5. Which is the Sahib's bungalow? 6. What is on the bank? 7. What is the price of this?

Exercise—6 (Page—12)

1. Ghar bhitra. 2. Mero ṭhouṉmā. 3. Uniharu timi lai parkhalān. 4. E sipahi haru rūṭ march mā jālān. 5. Hāmro jāhaj le dusman māthi bam pheklā. 6. Hāmi C.O. Sāhib ko pās das baje jāne chhāuṉ. 7. Ek *section* pahāṛ ma pojisan lelā. 8. Uniharu ū chholdāri māṉ holāṉ.

Exercise—7 (Page—17)

1. He came from our house. 2. Was he near the house? 3. He wants to write. 4. Where is the road to the city? 5. How long have you been living here?

Exercise—8 (Page—17)

1. Ū barīk mā roj jāṉdai na. 2. Taṉ aile hiṉris bhane wahāṉ sāṛhe āṭh bajī puglās. 3. Ū bimār chha bhane ū āune chhaina. 4. Ma kitāb bholi paṭhāuṉla. 5. Hāmi bajār jāne chhauṉ.

Exercise—9 (Page—26)

1. Timro bārik ma jāu. 2. Yo uslāi deu. 3. Mero ghar mā jāu 4. Jīt Bahadur kahāṉ chha? 5. Jaba Comanding sahab āunchhan malāi khabar dinu. 6. Mero pustak mā lekha. 7. Jawāb dinu ko aghi socha. 8. Dinai pichhe timi chaha piuchhau? 9. Hawaldar kahān baschha? 10. Ū

yahān basdāina. 11. Ū line mā baschha. 12. Usko ghar ko nambar kati ho? 13. Aba kahān janchhan? 14. Ma āfis mā jānchhu? 15. Bhare belukā hami wahān jāunla.

Exercise—10 (Page—26)

1. What is he saying? 2 What is it for? 3. Please send another man. 4. Is the man swift? 5. Let us hear now. 6. The roof of this room is leaking. 7. Whose turn now? 8. Ask different questions. 9. This has become rotten. 10. Go away.

Exercise—11 (Page 27)

1. He did it according to his own sweet will. 2. He gave me a bread. 3. When din he come? 4. He did it unknowingly. 5. I did bravery in the battlefield. 6. They drilled at '0800 hrs this morning. 7. Jem sahib told that the fellows ate their food. 8. He did not read his lesson yesterday. 9. He did not sleep last night. 10. He saw.

Exrcise—12 (Page—27 and 28)

1. Ma 5 baje station mā gayen. 2. Hijo kati baji āyeu? 3. Kasle yo chiṭṭhi liāyo? 4. Mussoorie mā timi kati din basyeu? 5. Bihana timi kahān gayeu? 6. Mr. John Lucknow mā ek haftā base. 7. H. Q. bāta kasle yo chiṭṭhi liāyo? 8. Kina 9:15 baji timi āyenau? 9. Urdu master āja āyenun. 10. Kati jānā sipahi chhuṭṭi mā gaye?

Exercise—13 (Page—31)

1. Uniharū station gaye kā chhan. 2 Kye timi le Bilāyet ma chiṭṭhi lekhe ka chhau? 3. Uni Kumāri Helen ko ghar mā gaye ki chhan? 4. Maile John lai dekhe ko chhu. 5. Ke usle jawāb liāye ko chha? 6. Ke timi le

mero chij-bij station bata liāyeu? 7. Ū chhuṭṭī ma gaye ko chha. 8. Ke damai (darzī) āyo?

Exercise –14 (Page—31)

1. Colonel had his inspection yesterday. 2. We faced a great number of enemies. 3. They marched 15 miles in 5 hours. 4. We had taken our food at 1000 hrs this morning. 5. Men have finished their work. 6. Did you hear the descriptions. 7. We have lost the money. 8. I have come. 9. Have you seen our army. 10. He might have gone to Delhi. 11. He has gone.

Exercise—15 (Page—32)

1. Maile uslāi hijo dekhe ko thiyen. 2. Ū dui din aghi āi puge ko thiyo. 3. Hijo āndhi āye ko thiyo. 4. Usle 6 mahinā samma paṛhe ko thiyo. 5. Uniharū le eotā lāmo chiṭṭhi belāyet mā lekhe ka thiye. 6. John le Henry lāi eota kitab diye ko thiyo. 7. Unihāru le khānā khāi sake ko thiye. 8. Usle dekhe ko thiyo.

Exercise –16 (Page—33)

1. Our people had dug the trench. 2. Colonel had agreed for furlough. 3. Gurkha units had fought well in Burma. 4. The cook had cooked the food. 5. I had seen him in Bombay.

Exercise—17 (Page—34)

He used to bring fresh news every day. 2. We were taking the wounded to the hospital. 3. Our men were on parade in this field. 4. What games were they playing? 5. Two years ago we were living in a big bungalow. 6. One soldier was on duty every night in this place. 7. I used to speak Gurkhali well before I went to England. 8. We used to go there often to look for enemies positions. 9. Where you living in the house in front of us? 10. When Capt. Hulse used to go there the people were very glad. 11. Colonel used to talk in Gurkhali to the soldiers.

Exercise—18 (Page 35)

1. The teacher will be teaching Roman-Urdu to the soldiers. 2. The horses will be grazing in the field. 3. The children must be playing in the field. 4. He must be coming from home. 5. Himmat Singh will be doing work uptill now. 6. The soldiers will be taking their food now. 7. British aeroplane will be bombarding the Germans. 8. Allen Sahib must be writing letters always to you.

Exercise—19 (Page 36)

1. If he had known the where abouts of enemies he would have surely given us the information. 2. If our soldiers had been here an hour ago, all of them would have been killed. 3. If we had not started at 2, o'clock we would not have reached there in time. 4. Had there been water in the stream there had been much difficulties. 5. If you had been able to speak Gurkhali, it would have been much easier for you. 6. If he had drunk the water of this well, he would have died. 7. If the enemies had been seen we would have sent the news. 8. Had there been no rain today we would have gone to Mussoorie.

Exercise—20 (Page—38)

1. Pick up that knife. 2. Drink all the medicine. 3. Get on to your work. 4. Send news immediately 5. Switch on the fan.

Exercise—21—(Page 39)

1. Ma timro pustak mez māthi rākhchhu. 2. John le mero lāgi chiṭṭhi lekhi diyo. 3. Usle eotá kitab bhuiṇ-mathi phāṇki diyo. 4. Usle usko dusman (satru) lāi māryo. 5. Colonel sāhib le bholi timiharū lai bayān garlān. 6. Jhattai lugā badli gara. 7. Keto ghoṛā bata laṛyo. 8. Uniharū le sabha ma bole.

Exercise—22 (Page—39)

1. He is able to do exercise. 2. This man is able to reach the top of the mountain. 3. You will be able to rest. 4. That soldier is able to swim. 5. Ram Lal is able to take something now.

Exercise—23 (Page—40)

1. Ma Gurkhali bhasa bolnu sakchhu. 2. Keto le yo pustak paṛhnu sakchha. 3. Mero bhai āja āunu sakena. 4. Uniharū kaile aspatāl janu saklān? 5. Usle gāṛi bhetnu sakdaina. 6. Malai chinnu sakchhau? 7. Timi le malai Gorkha line mā jāne bāṭo batāunu sakchhau? 8. Timi angreji ramrari bolna sakchhau? 9. Kati jānā le pauriera khola tarnu sakchhau? 10. Mero lāgi yo kam timi le garnu sakchhau?

Exercise—24 (Page—40)

1. I have finished my work. 2. How many times have we told him. 3. He has seen this play. 4. You have

already explained him everything. 5. People have reached their homes safely.

Exercise –25 (Page—41)

1. Manchhe harū le khai sake (bhiyāye). 2. Uniharule āfno kām sake ka chhainan. 3. Timro pareḍ sakeu (saki bhiyāyeu)? 4 Hāmro khānā hāmi 6 baji sakchhauṉ. 5. Timile āfno path sakeu?

Exercise – 26 (Page—42)

1. We want to defeat the enemy. 2. We want to destroy the city. 3. I want to take your permission. 4. Padam Singh want to go to bazar. 5. He wants to play hockey.

Exercise –27 (Page—42)

1. Ma uniharū lai hernu māṉgchhu? 2. Ma Nepal ko bhāshā sikhnu māṉgchhu? 3. E Gurkhaliharū Jāpānī saṉga larnu māṉgchhau. 4. Ke timi yo kitab paṛnu māṉgchhau? 5. Mero dāju Dilli mā jānu māṉgchha.

Exercise—28 (Page—43)

1. We used to go to his house daily. I used to go. 3. He used to see. 4. We used to write a letter to England weekly. 5. He used to stay at home. 6. They used to talk all day long. 7. They used to play two hours.

Exercise—29 (Page—43)

1. Har haftā usle belāyāt ma chiṭṭhī lekh thiyo. 2. Uniharū afis ma 10 baji āuṉthiye. 3. Hāmiharū dinai pichhe sāṉj mā tennis khel thiyeṉ. 4. John le din bhari kām garthiyo. 5. Ketā harū chholdāri mā sut thiye.

Exercise—30 (Page—44)

1. The train is about to arrive at the station. 2. He is about to go to the bazar. 3. Tej Bahadur is about to go to the hospital. 4. The boy is about to sleep. 5. My relatives are about to come here.

Exercise—31 (Page—44)

1. Mero pitaji (babu) āuna lai taiyār chhan. 2. Nani sutna lai taiyār chha. 3. Ū belāyat ma eota lāmo chiṭṭhī lekhna lai taiyār chha. 4. Uniharū dushman māthi hamlā garnu taiyār chhau. 5. Uniharū aba hiṛna lai taiyār chhau.

Exercise—32 (Page—44)

1. I am going. 2. If he wishes he can come here. 3. Capt. sahib is learning Gurkhali. 4. Give me some milk. 5. Did you bring newspaper? 6. Come this evening. 7. Clean your boots. 8. Brush your coat. 9. The book is on the table. 10. Wait for him.

Exercise—33 (Page—45)

1. Pustak mej mathi chha. 2. Hami Commanding sahib'ko pās ma 7 baji jāne chhauṉ. 3. Kitab harū ma bholi pathauṉlā. 4. Ū line ma saṉdai jānna. 5. Ke hāmi harū station jāuṉ? 6. Pāni pardai chha, Mussoorie na jāu. 7. Chāhā khānchhāu (Pīnchhāu?) 8. Bazār gayera è chiz-harū liāu. 9. Lugā pattiyāyera rākha. 10. Ū herna lai taiyār chha.

Exercise—34 (Page—45)

1. He came from our house *or* (He came after seeing our house). 2. If the men would have stayed here I would have made all the arrangements. 3. If he would be ready

I would call him to dinner. 4. How long have you been here? 5. I am sending your parcel. 6. He was seeing. 7. I heard him speaking. 8. Were you living in the house infront? 9. He will be coming from home. 10. Had you come I would have given a letter for him.

Exercise—35 (Page—45 and 46)

1. Kye usle jawāb liāye ko chha? 2. Damāi (Darjee) āye ko chha. 3. Hamile eotā chiṭṭhi lekhe kā thiyeuṉ. 4. Uniharū le āfno khānā khāi sake kā thiye. 5. Timi le malāi lekhe ko bhaye ma jawāb dine thiyeṉ. 6. Dehra Dun Lucknow bhandā thanda chha. 7 Yo sab bhandā rāmro kitab ho. 8. Ma timro kitab mej mathi rakhuṉ lā. 9. Mā Gurkhali bhāshā bolna sakchhu. 10. Usle dekhi sake ko chha.

Exercise—36 (Page—46 and 47)

1. We ought to have work hard. 2. He ought to keep his stores carefully. 3. Jit Singh ought to be punished. 4. He ought to perform his duties. 5. Havildar ought to have gone to the lines after 9, o'clock. 6. We ought to have received correct information. 7. Bahadur Singh ought to win 8. He ought to have done nice fooding arrangements. 9. He ought to have replied to his letter. 10. The soldiers ought to have charged with fixed bayonets.

Exercise--37 (Page--47)

1. I will have to be at the station quickly. 2. The soldiers will have to get up early. 3. We have got to clean our guns. 4. You will have to defeat the enemies. 5. Ram

Singh will have to be operated. 6. I have to fight with the enemy. 7. The soldiers have to finish their work. 8. Havildar will have to be supplied with accounts. 9. He will have to get through the examination. 10 Everybody will have to clean their guns today. 11. I have to take one month's leave. 12. Mohan Lal had to cross the river. 13. Ganga Singh had to run away from the city. 14. Gopal had to vacate his house. 15. Sohan had to jump over the wall.

Exercise—38 (Page—47 and 48)

1. Maile turantai garnu parchha. 2. Ū class mā āunu parthiyo. 3. Timi le bal le sake samma laṛnu parchha. 4. Uniharū 2 baji yāhān āunu parchha. 5. Timi le hukm mānnāi parchha. 6. John le ramro kām garnu parthiyo. 7. Maile eota chiṭṭhi lekhnu parne thiyo. 8. Timi higo wahān jānu parne thiyo. 9 Maile yo na garnu parthiyo. 10, Ū wahān ek hafta basnu parne thiyo. 11. Usle heṛnai chha. 12. Malāi station jānu chha. 13. Usle heṛnai parchha. 14. Uslai line ma jānu paryo. 15. Malai eota chiṭṭhi lekhnu paryo.

Exercise—39 (Page—48)

1. The tiger began to roar. 2. He started to go to the city. 3. Bahadur Singh began to take food. 4. He started to work. 5. I began to study my lesson since 2, o'clock.

Exercise—40 (Page—49)

1. I allowed him to go in the room. 2. They allowed John to learn Hindustani. 3. We allowed him to play

football. 4. You allowed him to read that book. 5. I allowed him to go because he was sick.

Exercise—41 (Page—50)

1. You will get two weeks leave. 2. How much money he gets? 3. How much salary she gets? 4. How much salary she gets? 5. He met me today. 6. I met him today. 7. Bring water for me.

Exrcise—42 (Page—50)

1. Food is necessary for everbody. 2. It is not good to hurt some body's heart. 3. It is necessary to work hard for the examination. 4. To speak truth is a very good thing. 5. It is not good to waste time.

Exercise—43 (Page—51)

1. I saw him sleeping. 2. He saw him running. 3. I heard them speaking. 4. Tej Bahadur saw him drinking. 5. I saw him writing a letter.

Exercise—44 (Page—51)

1. Maile uslai patra lekhe ko dekhen. 2. Usle uniharulāi mandar (church) ma bole ko sune. 3. Maile uslai sānjh ma bajār gaye ko dekhen. 4. Timile uniharulāi *football* khele ko dekhyo. 5. Jonn sāhib le Mrs. Jones lai nachnulai jāna lage ko dekhe.

Exercise—45 (Page—51)

1. It is necessary for him to go. 2. It is necessary for him to retreat. 3. It is necessary for him to play.

4. It is necessary for Jit Singh to come. 5. It is necessary for John sahib to appear in the examination.

Exercise—46 (Page—51 and 52)

1. Timilai station ma jarur jā̃nu chā̃hin chha. 2. Uniharulai lamo chiṭṭhī lekhnu chā̃hin chha. 3. John sahib lai daftar ma jarur ā̃nu chā̃hin chha. 4. Malai Colonel sahib lai dekhnu jururi chha. 5. Timilai kamti bhane ko dui ghanṭa sutnu chā̃hin chha.

Exercise—47 (Page—52)

1. He tried to see the Colonel sahib, but he could not see (him). 2. He tried to take away our people. 3. I tried to fire (the rifle). 4. We tried to find out the enemy. 5. I tried to speak the Gurkhali language.